T0266973

ADVANCE PRAISE FOR *BE BOLD TODAY*

"*Be BOLD Today* is a must-read for everyone who truly desires to thrive and live the life they want. Leigh's road map for how we can design and live our best lives is clear and concise. Leigh reminds us that throughout life, you have to be bold and brave and willing to take risks—and potentially fail before you succeed. It's time to get comfortable being uncomfortable!"
—Shelley Zalis, CEO of The Female Quotient

"Through *Be BOLD Today*, you'll discover the power of The BOLD Framework to ignite meaningful change in your life. This is not just a book; it's a road map to wholehearted living and the courage to show up as your truest self. Through the book you will embark on a journey of self-discovery and embrace the boldness within you."
—Claude Silver, chief heart officer of VaynerMedia and author of the upcoming book *Showing Up*

"*Be BOLD Today*, rooted in The BOLD Framework, is a beacon of inspiration and practical wisdom. With clarity and insight, Leigh Burgess guides readers through a transformative journey, empowering them to navigate the complexities of life with courage and resilience. A must-read for anyone seeking to unlock their fullest potential and live a bold life of purpose and impact."
—Lisa Sun, CEO and founder of Gravitas, and bestselling author of *Gravitas: The 8 Strengths That Redefine Confidence*

"The moment you begin to think and act bold in every area of your life is the moment you begin to witness just how powerful you truly are. *Be BOLD Today* will not only show you how, but it will transform your future. You will notice the difference in how you show up in the world after applying what this book teaches you, and so will everyone else around you."
—Simon Alexander Ong, author of *Energize: Make the Most of Every Moment*

BE
BOLD
TODAY

Unleash Your Potential,
Master Your Mindset,
and Achieve Success

BE
BOLD
TODAY

LEIGH
BURGESS

Library of Congress Cataloging-in-Publication Data available.
ISBN: 978-1-68555-243-5
Ebook ISBN: 978-1-68555-805-5
Library of Congress Control Number: 2024901409

Printed using Forest Stewardship Council certified stock from sustainably managed forests.

Manufactured in China.
Design by Carole Chevalier.

10 9 8 7 6 5 4 3 2 1

The Collective Book Studio®
Oakland, California
www.thecollectivebook.studio

To Jason and Mayah, my everything.
To my parents, sisters, and brother
for being my original #bold tribe.

CONT

PART 1: KICK-START YOUR BOLD JOURNEY

PART 2: BELIEVE

PART 3: OWN

ENTS

FOREWORD

BY BONNIE WAN,
AUTHOR OF *THE LIFE BRIEF*

I was on my own journey towards boldness when Leigh Burgess came into my life. I was immediately captivated by her story. Her rise from student athlete to the health care C-suite had the makings of a classic American achievement story. She had checked the boxes, scaled the peaks, and earned the accolades. Her career looked perfect on paper. Yet she found herself empty and exhausted—dancing on the edges of burnout.

But that wasn't the problem. The real challenge was what to do about it, if anything at all. Isn't this just a part of the unspoken job description for a modern-day leader with moxie? Isn't the remedy simple and the same as it's always been—a good night's sleep, so she can get up and go at the grind the next day?

Leigh's health care career skyrocketed as her health plummeted.

As a career strategist and author of *The Life Brief: A Playbook for No-Regrets Living*, Leigh's story was unsurprisingly familiar. I have met countless people climbing mountains at the cost of their relationships, self, and health, without a clear sense of why.

This is where Leigh's journey detours from others. She dared to own her circumstance, get clear on her values, imagine alternatives, and invest in herself. She put her health ahead of her hustle. And it began with the bold move of unplugging from the system. From there she created the space to rest, recuperate, then reimagine.

Leigh's story doesn't neatly fit our cultural mythology of boldness—pushing boundaries, defying expectations, challenging the status quo. Or does it?

What if pushing boundaries means to erect new ones—in service of our well-being? What if boldness equates to pause, not push? What if boldness looks different for each one of us, defined on our own terms? As Leigh has learned and lived, boldness has many faces and takes many paths. For some, boldness means leaning into "yes" and taking bigger swings. Yet for others, it invites slowing down, or like Leigh, stepping off altogether.

In the following pages, Leigh invites you to define what boldness means to you, why it matters in your life, and how you can harness it to awaken your sense of purpose and aliveness. Bold living is a conscious decision to take ownership of our lives, shed the shackles of fear, and steer ourselves away from the stories of others so that we can reimagine our own.

Whose story are you living? Is it yours, or someone else's? How could or would your life look if you harnessed your boldness to author a story and life of your making?

BOLD MEANS

"**Bold is chasing your goosebumps. Leap into new spaces anchored in the center of your being and fueled by the truth of your desires. When we give ourselves permission to pursue what we *really, really* want in life, we tap into and taste our aliveness.**"

—Bonnie Wan, author of *The Life Brief,* and partner and head of brand strategy at Goodby, Silverstein, and Partners

On *The Bold Lounge* Podcast

INTRODUCTION

Welcome to a journey of transformation and courage, where boldness is the key to unlocking your extraordinary potential through the changes you will intentionally make. As your coach and guide through the pages of this book, I am here to support, challenge, and inspire you as you embark on an extraordinary adventure to live your best bold life, starting today. This book is a personal coaching session extended across chapters, designed to lead you toward a life that's bolder, more authentic, and more aligned with your purpose and passions.

In fact, writing this book is part of my own bold journey. After twenty years of executive experience in health care and education, I launched Bold Industries Group (BIG). BIG supports organizations and individuals through consulting, coaching, and curated events, all with a spirit of boldness, meaningful connection, and purposeful direction. I developed The BOLD Framework over my decades of professional experience and now share its power with individuals and organizations ready to break free from mediocrity and leap into excellence.

Hosting *The Bold Lounge* podcast and creating The Bold Table, The Bold Retreat, Mindset Gym, and The Bold Leaders Collective are platforms for me to share my insights and catalysts for a movement of bold leadership, especially among women. While the principles of The BOLD Framework are universal, my focus on women has provided me with unique insights into their journeys of change. Their stories, which form the backbone of this book, are real-life examples that light the path to being bold. Women often navigate a whole host of societal pressures, making their willingness to change not just an act of boldness but also, sometimes, a necessary rebellion against the expected. I celebrate this spirit of change, acknowledge its complexities, and honor its transformative power.

As I have led BIG from a bootstrapped start-up to a successful business, I have lived these principles, and this journey has taught me that true boldness is an art and a science, a harmonious blend of intuition, intention, mindset, action, and strategy. I have also had the honor of inspiring thousands of women to create positive change using The BOLD Framework. I am thrilled to share these principles with you so that you, too, can step into your greatness. Be ready to challenge the status quo, defy limitations, and become the architect of your destiny.

THE BOLD FRAMEWORK:
FOUR STEPS TO ACCELERATE POWERFUL CHANGE

At the heart of your bold journey is The BOLD Framework, a powerful compass that will guide you as you navigate change and personal growth. As part of your bold journey, you will define what being bold means to you.

For me, boldness is *the courage to step forward and make changes, even when the path ahead may be shrouded in uncertainty.*

It's about trusting the intuitive spark within, even when doubts cloud the horizon. It requires facing challenges head-on, anchored in unwavering self-belief, even when external voices attempt to sway you.

However, The BOLD Framework is not just a methodology. It is a testament to the power of adaptability and the courage to evolve. On your bold journey of change, you will discover a pathway to personal transformation that is both practical and profound. You will be empowered to take control and make intentional choices that lead to a fulfilling and authentic life. You will integrate the insights and strategies you learn into a blueprint to make a change and reshape any area of your life you choose so that you can experience a newfound sense of thriving. This is not just about dreaming. It is about converting those dreams, aspirations, and goals into tangible realities.

Part of the beauty of The BOLD Framework lies in its adaptability. Everyone's journey is different, and this framework is designed to fit your unique goals, needs, and desires, helping you map out a path that is exclusively yours and aligns with your deepest values and ambitions. You will do this through four foundational steps: *believe* in your boundless potential, *own* every aspect of your journey, *learn* relentlessly, and *design* a life that echoes your highest aspirations. Let's take a high-level look at each foundational step.

STEP 1: BELIEVE IN YOUR POTENTIAL

Belief is the cornerstone of all your actions, and in this book you will unlock the power of self-belief. You will explore strategies to overcome self-doubt, cultivate a positive mindset, and see the unlimited potential that lies within you. This step is about setting the stage for growth, building the confidence needed to pursue your dreams, and understanding that the journey to boldness starts within.

STEP 2: OWN YOUR STORY

Owning your story means embracing your unique narrative. You will explore the chapters of your life, finding strength in the struggles, wisdom in the lessons learned, and joy in the triumphs. You will take full responsibility for your journey and become empowered to make choices that align with your true self. This is about writing your story with intention, courage, and authenticity.

STEP 3: LEARN CONTINUOUSLY

Learning is an ongoing, enriching process, and it's a rewarding part of your bold journey. You will explore new possibilities, challenge old beliefs, and open doors to new life milestones you may have not thought were possible. Whether you are addressing personal development, professional growth, better relationships, or new passions, your focus will be on using continuous learning as a tool for transformation and empowerment.

STEP 4: DESIGN YOUR BOLD LIFE

The final phase of your journey is designing a plan for the life you have always dreamed of. You will apply the insights and lessons learned from your journey. You will set goals, create actionable plans, and develop strategies to turn your dreams into reality. This is where your belief, ownership, and learning culminate in a life designed by you, for you— a life that is bold, fulfilling, and uniquely and beautifully yours.

HOW THIS BOOK IS ORGANIZED

This book is more than a guide. It is your personal road map to designing a life of boldness and purpose. Picture yourself on a profound journey, moving from preparation to actualization, as you progress through the five parts of the book. As you turn each page, envision yourself stepping closer to the life you have always dreamed of. This book is your companion on a journey to self-discovery and bold living. Get ready to be inspired, challenged, and transformed!

PART 1: KICK-START YOUR BOLD JOURNEY

Chapters 1 to 3 set the stage for your bold journey forward. Here, you will tune into your inner voice, define boldness on your terms, and shatter myths that may have held you back. Think of this as your launchpad, where you gear up for the incredible steps ahead.

PART 2: BELIEVE

Chapters 4 to 6 delve into the first foundational step of The BOLD Framework: *believe*. Prepare to create your belief map, uncover any belief conflicts, and set goals that will be your guideposts toward change and progress. This is where you build the foundation for the mindset essential for a successful journey.

PART 3: OWN

Chapters 7 to 9 dive into the second foundational step of The BOLD Framework: *own*. You will craft a Wheel of Ownership, redefine success on your terms, and chart your course to greater agency and confidence. You'll learn how to steer your journey with conviction and clarity.

PART 4: LEARN

Chapters 10 to 12 are all about the third foundational step of The BOLD Framework: *learn*. You will explore new horizons and grow through setbacks. It is a process of discovery, of setting new directions and bridging gaps. Imagine yourself as an explorer, charting unknown territories with excitement and curiosity.

PART 5: DESIGN

Chapters 13 to 15 focus on the final foundational step of The BOLD Framework: *design*. This is the culmination of your journey, where you will weave together your life plan, building momentum and detailing your action steps. You will balance what you have learned and what you aspire to achieve, crafting a life that aligns with your true self, not just in theory but in practice.

ACTIVITIES: HOW TO GET THE MOST VALUE

Each chapter has one or more activities designed to help you apply the principles in the chapter to your own life. At times, you may feel impatient with the process, just wanting to get things done. I assure you, though, that giving yourself the time and space to absorb their lessons will make it easier for you to sustain your bold journey and more likely that you will achieve the change you set out to effect in your life. This is the interactive heart of the book. While I understand the rush of daily life might tempt you to skim the activities, I encourage you to pause, grab a journal, and engage with them fully. Each activity is carefully crafted to complement the chapter's content and build upon each other. The activities will guide you toward the change you aspire to achieve. Think of this as a workout for your mindset—the more you put in, the more transformative the results.

Reflection is a powerful tool for growth, and many activities in this book are designed to prompt deep introspection. Keeping a journal for your thoughts and responses will help you track your progress and serve as a tangible reminder of how far you have come. From redefining boldness in your own words to crafting actionable plans, each entry will mark a milestone on your journey. As you progress, your initial thoughts might evolve. Writing these down will help you record that evolution and empower you to turn abstract goals into concrete steps.

YOUR PATH AHEAD

Your journey toward boldness is ongoing. It is a path of continual learning, growing, and evolving. You will employ resilience and adaptability as steadfast companions to maintain your dedication and momentum as you follow your bold life plan. Resilience will give you the strength to bounce back more easily from adversity. Adaptability will give you the flexibility to deal more adeptly with the inevitable changes in life. This journey is not about reaching a final destination but about enjoying and learning from the path itself.

Throughout this book, I will be right there with you, offering insights, asking challenging questions, and providing exercises to deepen your understanding and application of The BOLD Framework. Expect to reflect deeply and grow exponentially. Think of this book as your personal coaching session, extended over time, allowing you to revisit and reengage with key concepts as you evolve.

Your journey to a bolder, more authentic self starts here. You will unlock doors you never thought possible and take steps toward a life of purpose, passion, and bold action. Are you ready to begin this life-changing journey? Turn the page, and let's start this incredible adventure together!

Scan this QR code to access extra content, including resources and templates.

PART 1

KICK-START YOUR BOLD JOURNEY

Tune into your inner voice, define boldness on your terms, and shatter myths that may have held you back. This section is your launchpad. Here, you will prepare for the meaningful steps ahead, gaining insights and tools to navigate your path.

BOLD MEANS

"Taking opportunities where you can stretch, knowing that there are people around you, as well as your inner pilot light, to hold you up when it's needed."

—Claude Silver, chief heart officer at VaynerMedia

On *The Bold Lounge* Podcast

CHAPTER 1
THE JOURNEY STARTS WITHIN

"The boldest adventure is a journey inward, where the whispers of the heart become the roar of transformation."

Welcome to the first step of an extraordinary journey, one that begins within you. This book is more than just a guide. It is a conversation with your boldest possible self, rooted in The BOLD Framework's four foundational steps: *believe, own, learn,* and *design*. Here, change is not just a concept, but a vibrant, attainable reality and the connection to your truest potential.

I sense you are holding this book because something inside you is stirring, gently nudging you toward change, growth, courage, and the fulfillment of your dreams. A path uniquely yours, whispering promises of transformation. I believe you are here because a voice within you refuses to be silenced, compelling you to step boldly forward into the unknown, be audacious, and seize the life you have always envisioned. Your journey toward meaningful change starts right here, right now.

One of the greatest strengths of The BOLD Framework is its ability to adapt to your individual needs and aspirations. It is like guidance from a trusted friend, always matching your steps, big or small, with boldness as the goal. The BOLD Framework is a transformative guide designed to help you align with your goals, purpose, and passion. Each of its four key steps plays a crucial role in personal and professional development.

- Believe focuses on fostering self-confidence in your abilities along with understanding your beliefs and their roots.

- *Own* emphasizes taking responsibility for your life and actions, mastering your mindset, and shaping your future intentionally and purposefully.

- *Learn* advocates for continuous growth and learning from experiences, successes, and failures.
- *Design* encourages crafting a personalized road map to success and happiness.

In this chapter, you will tune into what is calling you—what perhaps needs a little more of your attention and may be just the thing you need to identify your bold goal. You will uncover the essence of listening to your inner voice, a guide to your true self and aspirations. You will also learn the importance of embracing change and intentional living, understanding that your roles, responsibilities, and dreams are not set in stone but can evolve. Finally, you will practice scripting your own life's narrative and acting with clear intention. This is a journey of empowerment and self-authorship of your life, future, and happiness.

LISTEN TO YOUR INNER VOICE

You may associate life changes with major events, dramatic turns, or life-altering moments. However, the true beginning of a transformative journey often lies in the most understated of moments—that inner spark to make a change.

Imagine yourself in a room full of noise, where every voice is competing to be the loudest. In that overwhelming chaos, you hear a faint whisper. The sound is not boisterous or forceful, yet it carries a weight of sincerity and truth. That whisper is your inner voice, your truest compass. It is a gentle nudge, urging you to realize your dreams. It is the voice of your aspirations, the spirit of your hopes, and the echo of your untapped potential calling. It's vital to practice paying attention to that inner voice, which will reveal what you truly want.

ACTIVITY
"I AM" STATEMENTS, PART 1

In this activity, you will practice listening to your inner voice without editing it. So often, we overthink or edit our thoughts, which may also mask our beliefs.

1. PREPARE
- Find a comfortable and quiet space.
- Grab a journal or paper and a pen or pencil.

2. SET A TIMER
- Set a timer for one minute. This time constraint is designed to encourage spontaneous and instinctive responses.

3. WRITE "I AM" STATEMENTS
- Begin each sentence on your paper with "I am . . ." and complete it intuitively.
- Leave a few lines of space under each statement. This is crucial for the next part of the exercise.
- Your responses can vary greatly. They might be self-descriptive (e.g., "I am creative"), emotional (e.g., "I am happy"), aspirational (e.g., "I am a future author"), or even whimsical (e.g., "I am a seeker of adventures").
- Do not limit yourself. The statements can be about your talents, actions, feelings, beliefs, accomplishments, or your current or future states of being.
- Write quickly, without pausing to think too much or edit. Allow your subconscious mind to guide you.
- Focus on the flow of your thoughts and keep your pen moving until the timer ends.

4. STOP WRITING WHEN THE TIMER RINGS

▶ Stop immediately. This helps maintain the authenticity of the exercise.

▶ Do not read or analyze your statements just yet. The next part of this activity will involve exploring these statements more deeply, but for now, give yourself a moment to transition from the writing phase to the reflective phase.

▶ Take a moment to breathe and relax. Reflect on the experience of free-flowing thought and self-expression.

By not editing what you write, you open a window into how you see yourself at a fundamental level, possibly revealing aspirations, values, beliefs, and facets of your identity that may be overshadowed by daily routines and external expectations.

ACTIVITY
"I AM" STATEMENTS, PART 2

Now that you have a list of your spontaneous "I am" statements, it is time to delve more deeply into understanding and interpreting these reflections of your self-perception.

1. ASSESS YOUR STATEMENTS

▷ Review each of your "I am" statements.

▷ Place a plus sign (+) next to each statement that represents a positive belief about yourself. These could be strengths, accomplishments, positive traits, or anything that makes you feel good about who you are.

▷ Place a minus sign (−) next to statements that seem to indicate a negative or limiting belief about yourself. These might include insecurities, doubts, or any aspect that you perceive as a weakness or a barrier.

2. ANALYZE POSITIVE BELIEFS (+)

▷ For each statement with a plus sign, take a moment to explore it further.

▷ Underneath each positive statement, write down ways you can continue to support or nurture this aspect of yourself. For example, if you wrote, "I am creative," list actions that could enhance your creativity, like dedicating time to your art or seeking new sources of inspiration.

▷ Reflect on how this positive belief supports your goals and aspirations. How does this aspect of your identity contribute to your success or well-being?

3. ADDRESS NEGATIVE BELIEFS (−)

⟩ For each statement with a minus sign, start by questioning its accuracy. Is this belief a true reflection of who you are, or could it be a distortion based on past experiences or external opinions?

⟩ List ways you might challenge, counter, or reframe this negative belief. For instance, if you wrote, "I am not good at public speaking," consider steps to improve this skill or ways to change your perspective about your abilities.

⟩ Reflect on how each belief might be limiting you. What opportunities or experiences are you potentially missing out on because of this belief?

4. REFLECT ON YOUR DISCOVERIES

⟩ After completing this analysis, take some time to reflect on the overall experience.

⟩ Consider what surprised you the most. Were there more positive or negative beliefs? Did you discover any hidden strengths or unrecognized challenges?

⟩ Think about how this activity might affect your self-awareness and self-esteem. How can you use these insights to foster personal growth or professional development?

This two-part activity will uncover your subconscious beliefs about yourself and encourage a deeper understanding of how these beliefs shape your reality. By categorizing and analyzing these statements, you can gain valuable insights into your self-concept, empowering you to reinforce your positive traits and address any negative perceptions that may be holding you back.

"In the journey to your best self, the most significant step is the one taken inward, where real change begins."

GIVE YOURSELF PERMISSION TO CHANGE

When considering a change, it is natural to seek external validation, to look to others to grant you permission to pursue your dreams. Yet, the profound truth is more liberating: the only opinion that truly matters is yours. Each morning, as you meet your own gaze in the mirror, remember that it is this person—filled with dreams, ambitions, and, yes, sometimes fears—who holds the key to your destiny. This reflection is intimate and knows every chapter of your life: the triumphs, struggles, desires, and experiences. Your task is to empower this reflection. In doing so, you align with the universe in a powerful collaborative effort to ensure you are making desired changes that move you forward in life.

Admittedly, the path to being bold is not easy at times and will have its challenges. Societal norms and personal fears can create formidable barriers. Doubts and insecurities, loud and insistent, may try to overshadow the quieter voice urging you to evolve. Questions like *Am I worthy? Can I truly succeed?* or *What if I stumble or, even worse, fail?* can anchor you in the safety of your comfort zone. However, recognizing these doubts for what they are—mere echoes of your apprehension—is the first step toward moving confidently out of your comfort zone and into your potential.

MEASURES OF BOLDNESS

There are several ways to measure being bold, and this list highlights the top six that I have found:

- **Risk-taking behavior:** Bold individuals are often willing to take risks and try new things.
- **Confidence level:** Bold individuals tend to have an overall higher level of confidence in their abilities and are not afraid to take on challenges.
- **Innovation:** Bold individuals often generate new and innovative ideas, products, or services.
- **Willingness to speak up:** Bold individuals are not afraid to speak up and express their opinions, even if they are unpopular or go against the norm.
- **Perseverance:** Bold individuals often persevere through challenges and setbacks, demonstrating a determination to achieve their goals.
- **Creativity:** Bold individuals often demonstrate a high level of creativity in their thinking and problem-solving.

ACTIVITY
EXPAND YOUR COMFORT ZONE

This activity will help you deeply explore your relationship with change, particularly focusing on your comfort zone and how it might be limiting your growth. It will encourage you to reflect on your openness to new experiences, consider your readiness to step out of your comfort zone, and identify specific areas where you might be holding back due to fear or uncertainty. By the end of this activity, you should have a clearer understanding of your own patterns and a plan for embracing change more readily.

1. SETTLE COMFORTABLY

▷ Find a quiet, comfortable space where you won't be disturbed.

▷ Have a journal and pen ready for jotting down your thoughts.

▷ Before diving into the questions, take a few moments to relax and center yourself. Breathe deeply and clear your mind.

2. ASK QUESTIONS ABOUT YOUR COMFORT ZONE

▷ Reflect on and write down answers to the following questions. Be as honest and thorough as possible.

Being Open to Change

▷ How am I open to change in my daily decisions?

▷ Can I identify moments when I embraced change recently? What was the outcome?

Pushing Boundaries

▷ What steps am I taking to push beyond my comfort zone?

▷ Are there new activities or hobbies I've tried or want to try? What's stopping me?

Avoiding Risk

▷ When have I shied away from taking a calculated risk?

▷ What fears or beliefs are associated with these situations?

Preparing for Future Opportunities

▷ How can I better prepare myself to embrace similar opportunities in the future?

▷ What practical steps can I take to build my confidence and risk-taking ability?

3. ANALYZE MORE DEEPLY

▷ Look for patterns in your responses. Are there specific areas where you consistently avoid risk? Are there certain types of changes that you embrace more easily?

At some stage in life, most people will grapple with imposter syndrome. It is that sneaky feeling where you question your own achievements, despite being skilled and experienced. This kind of self-doubt can really throw a wrench in your plans, especially when you are on the brink of choosing a path less traveled or going in a bolder direction. It is like an internal voice constantly questioning your worth, holding you back from stepping into new and exciting territories.

Society's expectations do not make it any easier, either. We all have these unwritten rules and ingrained beliefs, often shaped by stereotypes, which can quietly undermine our courage to pursue something different or daring. But here's the deal: When you decide to embrace change, it is more than just a decision. It is a declaration of self-trust. It is you telling yourself that you are worthy, capable, and ready to pursue your dreams. It is about stepping into your power, freeing and owning your boldness. That is the real game-changer.

"Embrace the beauty of becoming. The most powerful stories are those still unfolding."

MOVE FORWARD WITH INTENTION

In the journey of transforming your life, intention is your most powerful ally.

To be *intentional* is to make choices that resonate deeply with your truest aspirations, even when they challenge the status quo. Being intentional allows you to respond to life with purpose, not just react to what comes your way. Every step you take is deliberate, each decision steeped in awareness. These steps are not simply happenstance, but a conscious move toward the life you want.

Intentionality transcends being a mere strategy. It is a mindset, a guiding force. It is the underlying purpose that drives your decisions. It's easy to get caught up in the daily grind, operating on autopilot and losing sight of what you truly want. But remember, the essence of every choice, every action, is intention. When you embrace this mindset, you give direction to your life, navigating toward your goals with precision and clarity. Change is a constant, but when it is driven by intention, it becomes a powerful force for personal transformation, pushing you beyond the familiar confines of your comfort zone and leading you to new possibilities and growth.

"Bold is believing in yourself when others think you're crazy. Chase the dream, take the sabbatical, and follow the road that best suits you. Have no regrets when you look back, regardless of age. It's never too late to pursue your dreams."
—**Kelli Burke, VP of Commercial Multifamily Finance at Mortgage Bankers Association**

Here are some examples of how being intentional can affect life change:

- **Career shift:** Alice, a talented engineer, always felt a creative itch. Instead of ignoring that pull, she set an intention to blend her technical skills with her creative passions. She started taking design courses and, over time, transitioned into a role where she could use both her engineering and design skills by creating user-friendly software interfaces.

- **Health transformation:** Samantha had always struggled with her weight and fitness level. She made an intentional decision to understand her body and its needs. She consulted nutrition and fitness experts and created a personalized plan to implement healthier, sustainable lifestyle changes. She chose to be accountable to herself first and foremost.

- **Growth through travel:** Bri had always felt confined in her small hometown. She set an intention to explore the world. With careful planning and saving, she took a year to travel and work in various countries. She learned new languages, embraced different cultures, and gained a broader perspective. Upon returning, Bri started a community program, bringing together people from various backgrounds to learn from one another. Her intention not only transformed her personal life but also positively impacted her community.

As you progress through the chapters, here are some ways to integrate being intentional into your life:

- **Take time for self-reflection.** Set aside time each week to reflect on your actions, decisions, and feelings. Ask yourself, Are my actions, decisions, and feelings moving me toward my goals?

- **Visualize the outcome.** Before embarking on a new endeavor, picture the end result. What will achieving this goal look like? How will it feel? This visualization can serve as a motivator during challenging times.

- **Record your journey.** Throughout the book, you will pause at times to reflect, to take in the words and make them your own. I recommend that you keep a journal of your thoughts and feelings to record your bold journey.

INFUSING DAILY LIFE WITH INTENTION, TO BEGIN . . . BEGIN
Let's take a lighter-hearted look at being intentional in your day-to-day life.

Coffee conundrum: Imagine your daily morning coffee or tea. Are you routinely gulping it down? Instead, be intentional. Feel the warmth of the mug. Savor the aroma. Taste every sip. Take a moment to truly be present.

Closet clutter: Ever feel your closet is too cluttered or doesn't reflect who you are? Intentionally, think about your current life activities (for example, do you now work remotely?), style, comfort, and preferences. Maybe you will end up decluttering to opt for a minimalist look. Or maybe it's time to try something completely different that reflects your heightened boldness.

Digital detox: We have all been there, mindlessly scrolling. What if you choose more intentionally when and how to engage with the digital world? Maybe it's dedicating time for a nondigital hobby, like knitting or hiking; setting "no phone" zones in the house; or deleting apps that do not add value to your life. This makes the tech world less of a pull and more of a tool, serving intentional choices.

Vacation variations: Planning a vacation? Ask yourself, *What do I really want from this break?* Whether it is adventure, relaxation, culture, or a mix of everything, tailoring your vacation based on intention ensures not just great photos but also lifelong memories.

ACTIVITY
WHAT IS YOUR WHY?

Ask yourself, *Why do I want to make a change now? What prompted me to pick up this book and launch my bold journey?* Write about your motivations. As you move forward on your bold journey, you can refer back to these notes to remind yourself about the reasons you're seeking change. You can also see if your motivations evolve over time.

WRITE YOUR OWN SCRIPT

When embarking on the journey of change, it is essential to recognize the role of intention in shaping your life's narrative. Your life is not a prewritten screenplay where you are just an actor following a script. Rather, you are the writer, the director, and the lead actor of your own life. Every decision you make, big or small, is like writing a line, a scene, or even an entire chapter of your personal story. This concept might feel overwhelming, but it is also empowering. Consider this: Every day, you are presented with choices. Some of these are mundane, like what to eat for breakfast. Others will be more significant, like deciding on a career move or where to live. Each choice you make is a line of your story, your life.

"For me, bold means taking intentional actions to qualm the fear and persist in moving forward to reach a goal or dream, overcome unprecedented challenges, or better a situation. For me, it isn't about being 'fearless' or 'brave.' It's simply an unwillingness to be limited."
—Sarena Diamond, CEO and founder of Diamond Solutions Group

It is easy to fall into a routine, letting days, weeks, or even years pass in a blur, feeling like life is happening to you rather than you choosing to shape it. But the truth is, even in routine, there is a choice—the choice to continue as you are or make a change.

Your story so far might include chapters written under the influence of family expectations, societal pressures, or the impact of past experiences. These chapters are valuable. They have contributed to who you are today. But it is important to remember that they do not dictate the direction of your future chapters.

Christine was determined to become the first in her family to graduate from college, despite her father's opposition. After marrying, she worked at her husband's construction company. Following the birth of their daughter, Christine sought a stable job with benefits. Through a client's referral, she landed an interview at a local bank and was hired for an administrative position. "That got my foot in the door," she recalls. Taking full advantage of the bank's education benefits, Christine completed her degree at night. "I was proud to have my daughter witness my graduation," she says. "I taught her to keep her dreams alive and to persevere through any obstacles." Thirty-three years later, Christine is still at the bank, now serving as the executive vice president, chief credit officer, and COO of a subsidiary. "Keep reaching, and you will achieve," she advises.

As you turn the page to your next chapter, consider what you want it to say. Maybe you have always wanted to learn a new skill, like video editing or cooking, but never found the time. Or perhaps you have been thinking about a life change, like hitting pause on a relationship or making a career move. It is never too late to pause and reflect on what truly matters to you. You can pick up a pen and write these aspirations into your narrative. Dreams and goals do not have an expiration date. Your intentional choices today are crafting your story for tomorrow.

But how do you start? Begin by setting aside some time for introspection. What are your passions, values, and goals? What chapters in your life are you most proud of? What lessons have you learned from the challenges you have faced? Use these reflections to guide your choices moving forward.

Remember, being intentional does not mean you have to have it all figured out right now. It is okay to explore, try new things, and even fail. Each experience, successful or not, is a valuable part of your journey. The key is to keep moving forward, pen in hand, conscious of the power you hold in authoring your life's unique narrative.

ACTIVITY
UNVEIL THE DREAMS BEHIND YOUR BOLD STORY

This activity will help you tap into the depth of your aspirations, reconnect with your inner voice, and uncover the dreams that fuel your journey. It will help you transcend the boundaries of practicality and explore the full range of your desires, both big and small.

1. IMAGINE A WORLD WITHOUT LIMITS

- Find a comfortable and quiet spot where you can relax and think without interruptions.
- Close your eyes and take a few deep breaths to center yourself.
- Begin by imagining a world without any limits—a reality where obstacles, fears, and practical concerns do not exist. Picture yourself in this world and feel the freedom that comes with it.

2. EXPLORE YOUR DREAMS

▶ Now, with that sense of freedom and possibility, ask yourself: *In this limitless world, how do I see my life unfolding?*

▶ Think about both short-term and long-term scenarios. What are you doing? Who are you with? Where are you?

▶ Consider the following prompts to ignite your imagination:
- If I had all the resources and time in the world, what would I do?
- What have I always wanted to try but never had the chance to?
- What am I most passionate about?

3. RECORD YOUR BOLD DREAMS

▶ Open your eyes and start writing down everything that came to your mind. Don't filter or judge your thoughts. Let your desires flow onto the page. List everything, from grand life goals to simple joys and pleasures. This might include career aspirations, travel dreams, personal development goals, hobbies, and lifestyle changes.

4. EMBRACE THE IMPRACTICAL

▶ Challenge yourself to include dreams that may seem impractical or unrealistic. This exercise is about exploring possibilities, not confining yourself to what seems achievable right now. Remember that what seems impractical today might become attainable tomorrow.

5. REFLECT AND PLAN

▶ Once you have a comprehensive list, take some time to reflect on it. Notice any themes or patterns. Are there certain types of activities or goals that appear frequently?

▶ Think about how you might start to incorporate these dreams into your life. What small steps can you take today to start making these dreams a reality? Commit to making one of these small steps.

6. REVISIT YOUR LIST REGULARLY

▶ Revisit this list often. As you grow and evolve, so will your dreams. Update your list as new aspirations emerge and old ones are achieved or change.

This activity is not about daydreaming. It is about setting the stage for real-life changes and honoring your deepest desires. By listening to your inner voice and acknowledging what truly ignites your passion, you lay the groundwork for a bold, fulfilling journey ahead. Remember, the dreams you jot down today are the seeds of your future reality.

CLARA'S DISCOVERY

Consider the story of Clara, a living testament to the art of writing your own life story. For more than two decades, Clara worked successfully in the corporate world, her life revolving around board meetings, deadlines, and annual reports. But behind that business persona was a soul that yearned to be more creative and paint.

Art for Clara was more than just a hobby. It was her calling. Societal and familial expectations had nudged her toward the corporate world, but as years went by, the whisper from within to embrace her true passion grew louder. One day, driven by an unshakable belief in herself, Clara made a bold move. She said goodbye to her corporate identity and embraced her true self, an artist.

Her art studio, which started as a small space in her garage, has now blossomed into a place for art seekers and new artists alike. She felt bold because she believed in herself, embraced what she truly enjoyed, and took intentional steps to make it happen.

Writing her new life story did not mean she had to discard her past. Instead, she wove her experiences and skills into a broader picture that was more aligned with her true self. This type of intentional change doesn't erase chapters in your life but adds richer, more meaningful ones.

Such transformations do not occur in a vacuum. Clara's shift required immense introspection. She had to dig deep, understand her true desires, and differentiate them from fleeting thoughts. She faced her share of skeptics, moments of self-doubt, and inherent snags. But her clear intention and belief in herself propelled her forward.

If Clara's story teaches us anything, it is that writing a new chapter, though challenging, can be immensely rewarding. A bold move can lead you to a life that is not just lived but cherished, a life where each day aligns more closely with your truest self.

YOUR STORY CONSTANTLY EVOLVES

To author your own story is to embrace the possibility of growth and transformation at any stage in life. You are acknowledging that life is a dynamic story, one that you can enrich by having new experiences, learning, and exploring your purpose and passion. As you turn the pages of your life, each page is blank, awaiting your imprint. It bears no judgment, holds no grudges, and is receptive to what you want most in your life. It fuels your relentless spirit to grow and evolve.

As you stand ready to script your next chapter, understand that you are creating not just any narrative, but one that is written by you, for you, and all about you. Your journey is not a mere progression of days, but a sequence of growth, learning, and opportunity.

Your boldness is not defined by the size of your steps, but by the very act of moving forward, no matter how small or hesitant a step might seem. Boldness is in the courage to embrace the unfamiliar, challenge the status quo, question, seek, and take the next step, even knowing you might fail.

You might ask, "Where and when do I start on this journey of boldness?" The truth is, by picking up this book you have already taken the first step. The journey begins by tuning into your inner voice, that guiding force within you, and stepping forward with a clear intention. With every insight you gain and every intention you set, you are actively composing the next chapter of your bold, beautiful story.

KEY TAKEAWAYS

Listen to your inner voice. The quiet voice inside you represents your authentic self, your deepest desires, and your genuine aspirations. When you listen—truly listen—to that gentle whisper that nudges and encourages you, you amplify your power and trust in your capabilities.

Grant yourself the freedom to change. Life is not static, and neither should your dreams and ambitions be. Change your direction, aspirations, or dreams based on your evolving understanding of yourself.

Be intentional in your actions. Ensure that each step you take is intentional and act with purpose. Whether it is a career choice, a personal decision, or even a simple daily routine, move forward with clarity and intention.

Script your life's narrative. Life is about creating your own unique narrative. This involves consciously shaping your life story. You choose the chapters you want to include. Embrace the power of authorship. Remember that every day offers a new page on which to write.

WHAT'S NEXT

In chapter 2, you will embark on a crucial stage of your journey with The BOLD Framework. This is not just about understanding what boldness means in a general sense but about going deep to discover what it truly means to *you*. You will begin to pave your own path, one that resonates with your unique identity, aspirations, and values.

BOLD MEANS

"Bold is going out of your comfort zone and going somewhere no one else has gone before. Carving out a path where you are the pioneer."

—Charlene Li, author of *The Disruption Mindset*

On *The Bold Lounge* Podcast

CHAPTER 2
WHAT IT MEANS TO BE BOLD

"The essence of boldness is the quiet courage to be yourself in a world that constantly tries to shape you."

Boldness means different things to different people. For some, being bold could mean changing careers, speaking up publicly, or facing uncertainty head-on. For others, being bold is about quietly trusting their instincts amid life's noise. When you think of being bold, what comes to mind? Do you feel a surge of excitement, or do you encounter some hesitation? In this chapter, you will craft your own definition of what it means to be bold—one that resonates with your individual experiences and aspirations.

This is not about fitting into a predefined mold. Instead, it is about discovering how boldness looks and feels for *you*. Being bold is not always about grand gestures. Sometimes, it is about the small, consistent steps you take toward growth. It is about building self-belief and learning to trust your journey, even when it takes unexpected turns. This is your chance to redefine boldness in a way that aligns with who you are and who you aspire to be.

You will also explore strategies and insights to help you embrace boldness in your daily life. Whether you are taking your first steps toward change or looking to deepen your journey, this chapter is a starting point for a more intentional, confident, and bold approach to life.

BOLDNESS IS A CONTINUUM

Boldness often invokes images of grand gestures and earth-shaking decisions. Yet boldness, in its true essence, exists on a continuum. Bold can be quiet, a mild stretch, a big swing, or anything in between. It is a range of actions and decisions, from the subtle to the significant.

Sometimes, it is the whispers of courage that resonate the loudest.

Sometimes, the most meaningful expressions of boldness are the ones that do not make a big splash but instead create ripples of change in your daily life. It could be as simple as talking to your boss about a new idea, volunteering for your favorite charity, or adding a healthy breakfast to your morning routine.

QUIET BOLDNESS

On one end of the continuum are the quieter moments of boldness when courage may not be outwardly evident to the world yet holds personal significance. Boldness can be as quiet as a gentle push to try something new. Even the smallest acts of courage are significant.

In life, sometimes the most profound acts of boldness are the ones that do not make a sound.

They are the quiet choices you make every day, the ones that might not shake the earth but certainly shift the landscape of your life over time, and you determine the speed.

MILD STRETCH

Nestled at the heart of personal growth, there lies a sweet spot, a zone where you nudge yourself beyond the familiar, yet not so far as to be overwhelmed. It could mean making a conscious decision to extend your boundaries, just a bit more than you're accustomed to. Picture this: You are diving into a new project at work that is just outside your expertise, or perhaps you are picking up a new hobby that has always intrigued you, like photography or line dancing. Imagine, especially if you are an introvert, the quiet courage it takes to walk into a networking event solo. These steps, while they might appear small, are in fact bold declarations of your readiness to evolve. Each one is a venture into new, mildly uncharted waters, carried forward by a blend of curiosity, growth, and exploration.

BIG SWING

These are the leaps of faith where the decisions and actions significantly alter the trajectory of your life and usually have a considerable impact on others. This is where boldness roars, whether it is making a drastic career change, relocating, or investing your savings in a start-up idea. These moments, filled with both exhilaration and trepidation, require significant courage, resilience, and deep-seated self-belief.

Every shade of boldness, be it a whisper or a roar, represents a move, a change. Every point along the continuum holds value, reminding you that courage comes in many shades and intensities. It requires trusting your inner voice, no matter its volume, and realizing that even the quietest steps all the way to the loudest strides can have a significant impact.

"The boldest journey is the one that leads you closer to your true self."

MEET YOUR BOLD PERSONA

I kick off each conversation of my podcast, *The Bold Lounge*, by asking my guest one simple yet profound question: "What does bold mean to you?" The answers are as varied and as colorful as the guests themselves. The chart that follows captures recurring themes across their definitions of being bold. As you explore these themes, I invite you to reflect: Which of these definitions aligns with how you would define boldness? Which ones light up your imagination? Then, hold on to that spark of excitement as you dive into the activity that follows, where you will expand on your own unique take about what it means to be bold.

YOUR BOLD PERSONA

Theme	"I Am Bold When I . . ." (Action)	What I Would Think (Belief)	What I Would Say (Mantra)	How I Describe Myself When I Am Being Bold (Bold Persona)
Comfort Zone	Take risks and step into the unknown.	This may be unfamiliar, but it is the path to growth.	I embrace new experiences.	Pioneer
Courage and Fear	Act even when I'm afraid.	Fear will not stop me.	I feel the fear, but I do it anyway.	Brave Warrior
Authenticity	Live and act as my true self.	I am enough as I am.	This is the real me.	Authentic Soul
Agency and Decisiveness	Make decisions based on personal conviction.	I trust my judgment.	I believe this is right for me.	Self-Reliant
Facing Criticism	Stand by my choices, regardless of external feedback.	Others' opinions don't define me.	I respect your view, but I'm following my path.	The Original
Vision and Dreams	Pursue big, audacious dreams.	Anything is possible if I set my mind to it.	I have a dream, and I'm chasing it.	Visionary
Integrity and Empathy	Stand up for what's right, even when it's unpopular.	Doing what's right matters more than being popular.	Let's treat everyone with kindness and respect.	Compassionate Leader
Challenge to Status Quo	Forge a unique path, breaking conventions.	There's more than one way to do things.	I challenge the norm.	Innovator
Action and Movement	Proactively make things happen.	I am not a passive participant in life.	Let's do this!	Mover and Shaker
Responsibility and Impact	Work to better my community and the world around me.	I have the power to effect change.	We can make a difference together.	Changemaker
Trust and Faith	Follow my heart and intuition, even into the unknown.	I trust the journey, even if I don't see the destination.	I'm guided by my inner compass.	Faithful Explorer

BOLD PERSONA QUIZ

This quiz consists of questions to help you discover which Bold Persona best represents your approach to being bold. Answer yes for each question that most closely aligns with your feelings or actions. Say yes only when it represents you the majority of the time in your actions.

1 When facing an unfamiliar situation, do you feel excited about trying something new? **Pioneer**

2 Do you often act despite feeling fear? **Brave Warrior**

3 Do you find it easy to be yourself in various situations? **Authentic Soul**

4 When making decisions, do you primarily rely on your own judgment? **Self-Reliant**

5 Do you react negatively to criticism about your choices? **The Original**

6 Are you actively working toward a big dream or goal? **Visionary**

7 Do you strongly believe that community goals are just as important as your individual goals? **Changemaker**

8 Do you often stand up for your beliefs, even if they are unpopular? **Compassionate Leader**

9 Do you enjoy finding new and unconventional ways to do things? **Innovator**

10 Are you the person who initiates action in a group? **Mover and Shaker**

11 Do you actively participate in community service or social causes? **Changemaker**

12 Do you trust your intuition even when the path is not clear? **Faithful Explorer**

13 Are you comfortable with stepping out of your comfort zone regularly? **Pioneer**

14 Do you find strength in your fears and use them to move you forward? **Brave Warrior**

15 Is staying true to yourself a top priority for you? **Authentic Soul**

16 Are you confident in making quick and firm decisions? **Self-Reliant**

17 Do you maintain your course of action even when others disagree? **The Original**

18 Do you have long-term goals that you believe you will achieve? **Visionary**

19 Do you find yourself often advocating for fairness and empathy? **Compassionate Leader**

20 Do you enjoy challenging traditional methods or thoughts? **Innovator**

21 Do you often find yourself leading or doing the majority of the work in team projects? **Mover and Shaker**

22 Do you feel a strong sense of responsibility toward making a positive impact? **Changemaker**

23 Do you follow your heart, even when it means taking risks? **Faithful Explorer**

24 Do you find thrill in exploring the unknown? **Pioneer**

25 Do you wait for things to happen or make them happen? **Mover and Shaker**

26 Do you feel that facing your fears has made you stronger? **Brave Warrior**

27 Do you believe that being authentic is more important than fitting in? **Authentic Soul**

28 Do you believe that when it comes to your life path, the only voice you need is your own? **Faithful Explorer**

29 Do you prefer to rely on yourself rather than others to make important choices? **Self-Reliant**

30 Do you stand firm in your beliefs, even under social pressure? **The Original**

31 Do you dream big and have a plan to make your dreams a reality? **Visionary**

32 Do you strive to be empathetic and ethical in all your actions? **Compassionate Leader**

33 Do you take the initiative to start new projects or suggest new ideas? **Innovator**

Scoring: For each question where you answered yes, give yourself a point under the Bold Persona it aligns with. For example, if you answer yes to question 1, give yourself a point under Pioneer. The Bold Persona with the most points represents your dominant style of boldness. If you have a tie, it indicates a blend of Bold Personae, reflecting your multifaceted approach to being bold.

EMBRACE YOUR BOLD PERSONA

This activity will deepen your understanding of your unique brand of boldness, helping you recognize and celebrate your strengths. By identifying with a Bold Persona and linking it to your personal experiences or aspirations, you gain insights into your character, natural bold tendencies, and potential for growth. This reflective process empowers you to embrace and express your boldness in everyday life where you are actively shaping your narrative.

1. REFLECT ON YOUR BOLDNESS

▸ Think about moments in your life when you have displayed boldness. This could be when you took a risk, stood up for your beliefs, ventured into unknown territory, or trusted your instincts in challenging situations.

▸ Write down a list of these moments to help you connect with your inner boldness.

2. UNDERSTAND THE BOLD PERSONAE

▸ Familiarize yourself with the different Bold Personae listed in the chart.

3. SELECT YOUR DOMINANT PERSONA

▸ Choose the persona that you most strongly identify with or aspire to emulate.

▸ Consider which traits align with your personal experiences or goals.

▸ If more than one persona resonates with you, try to determine which is most dominant in your life or which you wish to develop further.

4. REFLECT AND WRITE

▷ Once you have chosen your Bold Persona, reflect on why this particular one speaks to you.

▷ Write a short narrative or bullet points about a specific instance where you embodied this persona or describe how you plan to embody these qualities in the future.

▷ Try to connect the abstract concept of boldness with tangible actions and goals in your life.

5. REVIEW AND PLAN

▷ Look over what you have written. How do these reflections make you feel about your personal journey and potential?

▷ Use this insight to plan small steps or set goals that align with your chosen Bold Persona. This could involve personal development, career aspirations, relationships, or hobbies. Choose one small first step and commit to it.

6. SHARE AND DISCUSS (OPTIONAL)

▷ If comfortable, share your reflections with a friend or mentor to provide additional insights and encouragement.

By completing this activity, you are actively shaping your narrative of boldness. This is a journey of acknowledging your strengths, understanding your potential, and setting the stage for future growth and self-expression.

"Your boldness is your signature—unique, irreplaceable, and entirely your own."

Moving forward, embrace your Bold Persona in daily life. When faced with decisions or challenges, think about your persona's belief and mantra. Let them guide and inspire you to live out your boldness authentically. Remember, as you grow and evolve, so might your Bold Persona. Feel free to revisit this activity periodically to see if a different Bold Persona resonates with you.

DEFINITIONS OF BOLDNESS

Boldness is embracing the uncertain and challenging aspects of life, the steps that offer no promises of success yet are crucial to what lies ahead. This concept of boldness is not about reckless courage, fearlessness, or bravery. It is a thoughtful step into the unknown, grounded in the belief that there is immense value in each experience, regardless of its outcome.

In every bold step, there is a lesson to be learned, an insight to be gained.

MY DEFINITION OF BOLD

As I said in the introduction, for me, boldness is *the courage to step forward and make changes, even when the path ahead is shrouded in uncertainty.* It's about trusting the intuitive spark within, even when doubts cloud the horizon. In embracing this definition of boldness, I acknowledge that the journey itself, with all its ups and downs, is just as important as the destination.

I often find that true happiness stems not simply from making desired changes and achieving goals, but also from the very act of pursuing a path that aligns with my inner purpose and passion. Boldness is being in harmony with my deepest aspirations, even if it means facing discomfort or uncertainty. This alignment brings a sense of fulfillment that goes beyond conventional success. It lets me grow, evolve, and continually reshape my life's narrative in a way that resonates with who I am and what I stand for.

YOUR OWN DEFINITION

Creating your own definition of boldness is an empowering exercise that requires introspection and courage. Boldness is not a static concept, universally applicable. It is deeply personal, fluid, and evolving. To define it for yourself, consider your values, strengths, goals, and aspirations. What does being bold mean to you? Is it about taking risks, stepping out of your comfort zone, or standing up for your beliefs? Maybe it is about pursuing your passions relentlessly or choosing authenticity in a world that often favors conformity.

Reflect on moments in your life when you felt truly alive and in alignment with your deepest self. These moments hold clues to your unique and original brand of boldness. Crafting your definition does not mean adhering to societal standards or mimicking others' paths. It requires listening to your inner voice and honoring your journey. This personalized understanding of boldness will become your compass, guiding your decisions and actions, helping you live a life that is successful by your own standards and also deeply fulfilling.

ACTIVITY
DEFINE BOLDNESS FOR YOURSELF

In this activity, you will articulate your own definition of boldness. This personal definition will guide you as you navigate through The BOLD Framework and apply its lessons to your life. This makes the concept of boldness tangible and relevant to your firsthand experiences and aspirations. Such self-reflection sets a foundation for the subsequent chapters, where you will further explore and apply your definition of boldness.

1. REFLECT: Take a moment to think about what boldness means to you. Consider your past experiences, your values, and how you see boldness manifesting in your life.

2. WRITE: Jot down your thoughts and definition. This can be in the form of a list, a paragraph, or even bullet points. Try to capture what boldness truly means to you personally.

3. REVISIT: Keep this definition handy as you progress through the book. After completing key chapters or sections, return to your definition and think about how boldness shapes your thoughts, decisions, and actions. Reflect on whether and how your understanding of boldness changes over time.

By the end of the book, your personal definition of boldness will most likely have evolved and deepened. This activity is not just a onetime reflection but a continuous exploration of how boldness shapes your thoughts, decisions, and actions throughout your life's journey, making the concept of boldness a living, breathing part of your everyday experience.

KEY TAKEAWAYS

Boldness is a continuum. Bold actions range from small, personal acts of courage to significant life-impacting decisions. Appreciate all expressions of boldness, no matter their size, as valuable steps that contribute to your personal growth.

Embrace your Bold Persona. Identify and actively embody your bold qualities. Applying them in daily life leads to acting with more authenticity and confidence. This approach empowers you to face challenges and seize opportunities with self-assurance and strength.

Face uncertainty head-on. To me, boldness is the audacity to step forward, even when the path ahead is shrouded in uncertainty. This means having the courage to embrace risks and face unknown outcomes with a resilient spirit.

Your definition of boldness matters most. Your definition of boldness is deeply personal. It is your unique signature. This definition guides your decisions, shapes your actions, and influences how you navigate life's challenges and opportunities.

WHAT'S NEXT

It is crucial to distinguish between what boldness truly represents and the myths that frequently distort its essence. Chapter 3 debunks common myths, shedding light on the truths that popular beliefs and stereotypes often mask, which can cloud our understanding of boldness.

"Turn 'What if?' into 'Why not?'
with the power of boldness."

BOLD MEANS

"Finding my power, claiming my power, owning it, and holding on to it."

—Mita Mallick, *Wall Street Journal* and *USA Today* bestselling author of *Reimagine Inclusion*

On *The Bold Lounge* Podcast

CHAPTER 3
FIVE BOLD MYTHS DEBUNKED

"Boldness is not the absence of fear, but the triumph of will over the whispers of doubt."

Now that you have spent some time thinking about what boldness is and defining it for yourself, let's also consider what it is *not*. This chapter explores common myths about boldness that can hold you back. It is a bit like having static on a radio, distorting the song that is playing. So, let's clear the air. By understanding and dispelling these myths, you will be better equipped to rock your own kind of bold without any doubts holding you back.

MYTH #1: YOU MUST BE FEARLESS TO BE BOLD

We live in a world where strength and fearlessness are very often overdramatized. The image of the hero who forges ahead without a hint of fear is deeply ingrained in the cultural narrative. From movies to motivational seminars, the message is consistent: To be bold, you must be fearless. This is a myth. This flawed idea can discourage you from taking bold steps in your life, because you may think that your natural fears are a sign of weakness or inadequacy. The journey of the bold is not one of fearlessness but one of resilience, courage, and unwavering self-belief.

FEAR IS NATURAL

Boldness is not an inherent trait that only a select few possess. Rather, it is a choice you make, a conscious decision to act even when your instincts tell you to retreat. It can be gut-wrenching to push through feelings of uncertainty and rely on your convictions. You may still feel fear, but you choose to proceed despite it.

Fear is natural and an often-justified reaction to something unknown. It is not a sign of weakness. At its core, fear is a primal, protective mechanism. It is the body's way of signaling potential danger, making you more vigilant, thoughtful, and ready to react. Today, while most of our fears might not be life-threatening, they still play a crucial role in our decision-making. Being able to admit and acknowledge fear is a strength. It requires self-awareness and honesty. With today's pressure to strive for perfection, simply admitting fear can be a bold act in itself.

LEARN HOW TO MANAGE YOUR FEAR

Boldness requires courage to proceed in spite of your fears. Navigating fear is not about eradicating it but learning to coexist with it. You can recognize that fear is a part of the journey and develop strategies to minimize its influence. Because managing fear is so integral to being bold, we will explore ways you can do this throughout the book. Whatever the approach, the goal remains the same: to not let fear unduly influence your choices.

Let's look at an example. Imagine, after years of hard work, you have finally achieved the promotion you have long wanted. But the reality is far different from the dream you had. You are on top of your professional game, but it feels like you have no time or energy for anything outside work, including family and friends. This promotion, which once seemed like the pinnacle of your aspirations, feels hollow and lonely. Instead of basking in your achievement, you are overwhelmed by the weight of the responsibility and the realization that this is not what fulfillment feels like.

Taking a bold step, you decide to redefine your role. You set new boundaries, prioritize leadership over micromanagement, and delegate tasks to the capable team around you. Many would fear the potential backlash or perceive it as a sign of incompetence. But you recognize the true essence of bold leadership, understanding that saying no is as powerful as saying yes. By empowering your team, you also provide growth opportunities for others, fostering a positive work environment. This is not a move of fear or weakness. It is a bold statement that personal well-being and professional success are not mutually exclusive.

MYTH #2: A BOLD ACT IS BIG AND LOUD

In today's fast-paced, hyperconnected world, there is a notion that equates loudness and reach with power and significance. The brightest neon sign, the loudest voice in the room, the boldest statement— these are the things that capture the most attention. However, such a perspective leads to a dangerous misconception about the nature of boldness, that only big and loud acts can be considered bold. Let's dispel this myth.

BOLDNESS EXISTS ON A CONTINUUM

As we discussed previously, boldness ranges from quiet to loud, from introverted to extroverted, from feeling vulnerable to feeling invincible—and everywhere in between. It is a fluid trait that is often context dependent. Sometimes, it may manifest as a courageous decision. Other times, it might be a positive push outside your comfort zone.

Believing that a bold act must be big and loud may limit your interpretation of what it means to be bold. You may perceive your subtle, understated acts of boldness as lesser, thereby undervaluing your strengths and capabilities. You may also fail to recognize and appreciate the bold steps others are taking, simply because they are quieter and lacking the spotlight.

BOLDNESS IS AUTHENTIC SELF-EXPRESSION

Boldness stems from a place of conviction, from standing firm in your beliefs, even in the face of opposition.

Often, the quiet acts of boldness are driven by genuine authenticity and make the most impact, especially when smaller acts are additive.

Imagine being a team's leader when upper management pushes for layoffs. Knowing the value of your team members, you decide to push back with other options. You prepare a well-researched proposal, pointing out alternative budget cuts that will not affect your team's livelihoods. This is undeniably bold, as you are proposing an unrequested alternative, but you know it is the right thing to do for your team.

In the realm of personal relationships, it is natural to sweep issues under the rug, fearing confrontation. Recognizing that something feels misaligned and taking steps toward resolution requires boldness. For instance, you might realize that a long-term friendship has been strained and, instead of letting it fade away, you take the initiative to communicate and work toward rebuilding the bond.

Boldness is not confined to the loudness of your actions. Boldness can be found in the gentle whispers of your convictions, the subtle nods to your authentic self, and the quiet defiance against societal norms.

Both the introverted thinker who challenges tradition and the extroverted leader who inspires change embody boldness.

There is no right volume for boldness. It is the intent, the authenticity, and the courage behind the act that matter the most.

MYTH #3: IT IS TOO LATE TO BE BOLD

As time passes, it is easy to continue doing what you are doing, rather than making changes. This can happen even if what you are doing is not aligned with your passions or purpose. Societal norms can make change even harder by associating certain milestones with specific ages. However, the idea that it is too late to be bold, chase a dream, or change paths is a myth. Let's shed light on the timeless nature of boldness.

BOLDNESS DOES NOT HAVE AN EXPIRATION DATE

It is easier to stay in your comfort zone than to try something new, but that doesn't mean you cannot change. Over time, falling into routines and staying within the confines of your comfort zone can easily become a natural, almost unconscious habit. The daily grind, the familiar patterns, and the predictable outcomes provide a sense of security and stability. The idea of stepping outside this comfort zone can be daunting, sometimes to the point of feeling impossible.

You might catch yourself thinking, If I haven't made a change until now, it's unlikely that I ever will. This mindset, while understandable, is inherently limiting. It is a trap that convinces you that your past behaviors are definitive indicators of your future potential. This belief creates an invisible barrier, holding you back from exploring new opportunities and experiences. The comfort zone, though safe, often becomes a silo of stagnation, preventing growth and learning. It's important to recognize that this mindset is not a reflection of your true capabilities, but rather a common defense mechanism against the unknown.

Breaking free from this mental framework requires a conscious shift in perspective.

Every day presents a new opportunity to make different choices.

Your past does not dictate your future. The journey of change and personal growth is not restricted by age, past experiences, or current circumstances. It is a continuous process, always within reach. The key is to start with small, manageable steps that gradually push your boundaries. Over time, these small steps can lead to significant transformations, proving that it's never too late to change.

Too often people use the passage of time, such as age or tenure, as a reason not to take a risk or try something new. From a young age, society typically programs us to follow a linear path—get an education, secure a stable job, start a family, retire. While these are worthy pursuits, the idea that everyone should accomplish them in a specific sequence and time frame is restrictive and, quite frankly, outdated. If you venture outside established milestones and timelines, you may face skepticism or even discouragement. This experience can lead to an ingrained belief that opportunities for boldness diminish as the years go by. It simply is not true.

BOLDNESS IS A MINDSET, NOT A TIMEBOUND OPPORTUNITY

Boldness is not tied to your biological age or the number of years you have spent in a job or relationship.

Boldness is a frame of mind.

Every stage of life offers opportunities for growth and adventure. Recognizing and seizing these moments requires a bold spirit.

Boldness is not reserved for the young or the early stages of life.

It is a flame that can be ignited and rekindled at any moment. Your age, tenure, or past should never be barriers but rather sources of wisdom and experience that empower you to make bold decisions.

Consider Lisa's journey. She had a successful, decades-long career in the corporate world as a health care executive. However, as she neared retirement, she felt an unyielding curiosity to explore art and consider how she could take on a professional role in the art world. Rather than retire and pursue personal hobbies, Lisa embraced her passion by launching a company that sold one-of-a-kind gifts made by artists around the world. Despite starting from scratch in a new industry, her drive, experience, and passion led to her success. Her story stands as a testament that it is never too late to pivot, pursue your passions, and make bold choices.

DEVELOPING NEW SKILLS IS A LIFELONG OPPORTUNITY

Perhaps you want to learn to sing or play a musical instrument, yet the fear of judgment or the notion of not having natural talent holds you back from exploring this interest. However, many skills can be nurtured over time with the help of a teacher or even online classes.

The process of learning, practicing, and evolving is a bold journey, regardless of the final destination or achievement. Progress over perfection is bold.

Similarly, the way people interact in relationships can fall into a set pattern, leading to a feeling of stagnation. Yet, the beauty of human connections lies partly in our capacity to grow and evolve. Instead of settling for the status quo, you can rejuvenate a bond by learning new communication skills and exploring new experiences together. This applies to all sorts of relationships, including with significant others, friends, family, and colleagues. Embracing change in a relationship, especially after years of familiarity, is a bold act, signifying the commitment to continually cherish and nurture the bond.

MYTH #4: BEING BOLD IS LEAPING WITHOUT LOOKING

In many movies and stories, the protagonist will, on an impulse, make a seemingly big decision that dramatically changes the course of their life. These tales are captivating and exciting, and the audience often applauds such brashness as boldness. The reality, however, is different. True boldness does not mean taking action without weighing the consequences. It is not a spontaneous leap into the unknown. Let's dismantle this myth and highlight the conscious and intentional nature of true boldness.

BOLDNESS IS STRATEGIC AND PRAGMATIC

Genuine boldness is pragmatic and thoughtful.

Boldness is the result of intentional action and calculated, courageous risk.

Just as a pilot would not fly without ensuring the integrity of the plane and checking the weather forecast, true boldness also requires preparation. You consider the consequences and the effects on yourself and others. The steps are thoughtful and purposeful, and they take into account potential risks.

Boldness can coexist with risk in a thoughtful way through assessment and risk management.

Risk is a natural part of life and growth. However, the key is to take risks that are calculated, where the potential benefits outweigh the negatives, and you are prepared to handle possible setbacks. The essence of boldness lies in navigating these risks consciously and strategically.

Consider the realm of professional ethics. Reporting unethical behavior, especially in established institutions, can be daunting. There are potential repercussions, ranging from being ostracized to facing professional consequences. For example, Asmita had a stable job and witnessed unethical workplace practices. But instead of impulsively confronting her superiors, she meticulously documented everything, consulted legal experts, and approached the situation with prudence. When she reported the unethical acts, she was equipped with evidence and a strategy.

Or consider a transition from a full-time job to a part-time one. Quitting sounds like a bold step, and it is. However, boldness in this context does not mean impulsively resigning. It involves upfront work to figure out the details, understand the impact (including the financial implications), and do a reality check. For example, you may start out by taking on freelance projects or a new side hustle alongside your full-time job. This approach allows you to gauge the feasibility of a full-time freelance career while still having the safety net of your regular job.

BE CONFIDENT IN THE FACE OF SKEPTICISM

Some bold moves, such as pursuing higher education or changing career tracks later in life, can attract skepticism. Imagine you are in a technical role, but you aspire for a shift toward a more business-oriented position. Getting an MBA seems like the right step. However, some people might express doubts, reminding you of the costs and questioning the utility of such a decision at this stage in your career. True boldness does not mean ignoring these concerns. Instead, you'd research the return on investment of an MBA, understand the logistics, and consider the long-term benefits. After doing the research, you could then move forward with conviction.

Boldness is not a wild guess. It is a calculated stride into the future.

You recognize opportunities, understand challenges, and make decisions that align with your values and long-term vision. Such a step requires confidence—not in the absence of fear, but in the face of it. Being bold does not mean that you impulsively jump without looking. Instead, after carefully weighing the challenges, you decide to jump anyway, acting with intention and purpose.

MYTH #5: BOLD PEOPLE ARE ALWAYS CONFIDENT AND WITHOUT DOUBT

Imagine the typical picture of a bold figure. Who comes to mind? Are they standing tall, chin up, always certain about their choices, never faltering, and never second-guessing? This is the image often portrayed in the media and a misconception many people hold. However, reality paints a different picture. Let's explore the complex relationship between boldness and confidence and debunk the myth that they are always interconnected.

BOLDNESS AND CONFIDENCE ARE NOT NECESSARILY INTERTWINED

Boldness is not synonymous with steadfast confidence. On the contrary, many bold decisions are accompanied by a whirlwind of emotions, including fear, doubt, and vulnerability. The hallmark of a truly bold individual is not an absence of these feelings but the ability to move forward despite them.

While confidence can facilitate bold decisions, it is not a prerequisite.

Often you just have to take a deep breath and step forward anyway, even when the path is not clear.

Consider the story of Kelly. Her journey to write a book came with its own set of apprehensions. Her day job was a director for a shipping company. She got a shot of confidence when a publisher gave her a contract. Then came the hard part—actually writing the book, something she'd never done before. She worried about whether the content was compelling enough. She wondered whether the message would resonate with readers. Kelly's self-confidence took a hit as she grappled with these feelings of inadequacy. Yet, she persevered, driven by her belief in her message. The result? Her book not only elevated her career but also made a profound impact on countless readers.

"I think of bold as being vibrant and determined to do *the thing* even when you might not be fully certain or confident. Doing it with shoulders back, head up, and a deep breath!"
—Eden Ezell, chief compliance officer

ACTIVITY
EMBRACE BOLDNESS AMID UNCERTAINTY

In this activity, you will explore how boldness and confidence are not necessarily concurrent. Sometimes, acts of boldness emerge from moments of doubt.

Think of a time when you felt uncertain but had to choose a path. What did you feel? Was it fear, excitement, doubt, or a mix of emotions? Write about this experience, detailing any external challenges and internal emotional feelings. Highlight the moments when you felt the least confident yet chose to act anyway. While you are writing, look for moments of quiet boldness.

Having recognized your moments of quiet boldness, do you feel more empowered to act boldly in the future, even in the absence of unwavering confidence?

REFLECT ON HOW MYTHS AFFECT YOUR THINKING

In this chapter, we explored and contrasted what boldness is and what it is *not*, despite common misperceptions. Did any of these common myths, summarized in the Key Takeaways that follow, resonate with you? Consider looking back at your personal definition of boldness from chapter 2 and seeing if you now have a more expanded perspective on how you view boldness.

KEY TAKEAWAYS

Fear is part of the process of being bold. Being bold does not mean you are without fear, but rather that you act even when you feel fear.

Boldness is not always a loud, headline-grabbing move. Sometimes, the most meaningful acts of boldness are the ones that are done quietly.

Timing is not a barrier to boldness. There is no expiration date for making bold changes and brave choices in your life.

Being bold is not about rushing in without thinking. It is about sizing up the situation thoughtfully and then taking calculated risks.

Boldness and confidence are not the same thing. You can be filled with doubts and still make a bold move, all because you decide to push through and take action.

WHAT'S NEXT

Part 2 launches the first foundational step of The BOLD Framework: *believe*. You will explore how understanding boldness dovetails with the power of your beliefs. If you thought understanding your definition of bold was powerful, wait until you dive into how your beliefs can either energize your boldness or hold you back from your highest potential. Let's unlock the impact of what happens next when you not only act boldly but also truly believe in your actions.

PART 2

BELIEVE

In the next three chapters, we will delve into the first foundational step of The BOLD Framework: *believe*. Prepare to create your belief map, uncover any belief conflicts, and set goals that will be your guideposts toward change and progress. This is where you build the foundation for the mindset essential for a successful journey.

BOLD MEANS

"Being bold means that you have the courage to do the things that you really want in life. My formula for courage is self-belief that leads us to take action and then evaluating the results of those actions from a place of strength, to learn, not to regret, to convince ourselves to do it all over again. You have to believe in yourself first if you want to take that step to do something really bold in life."

—Lisa Sun, CEO and founder of Gravitas and author of *Gravitas*

On *The Bold Lounge* Podcast

CHAPTER 4

EXPLORE YOUR BELIEFS AND VALUES

"Belief propels boldness."

Thus far on your bold journey, you have practiced listening to your inner voice, clarified your personal definition of bold, and learned about five debunked myths surrounding boldness. Hold on to those building blocks and insights tightly. They pave the way to our next pivotal topic: our beliefs.

Within The BOLD Framework, *believe* is the first foundational step, a major structural element of implementing change in your life. Envision your beliefs as the foundation on which your habits, intentions, and actions reside. In this chapter, you will explore what your beliefs mean, where they come from, and why they are vitally connected to how you live your life. You will also experience the magic that happens when you say, "I believe."

WHAT IS A BELIEF?

A belief is a firm, unyielding faith or confidence in yourself, your ideas, or a vision for the future. Beliefs are more than just opinions or passing thoughts. They are deeply ingrained convictions. Whether you are aware of them or not, your beliefs guide your thoughts, feelings, and actions. They underpin every decision you make.

From the time you enter the world, you begin to absorb beliefs that shape your perspective and influence your choices. The ideas and values instilled in you by your parents, teachers, and society (for instance, through media exposure) play a significant role in molding your worldview. For example, your parents may have taught you that hard work always pays off. As a result of your belief that this is true, you work hard to meet your goals. You might, however, harshly judge others who seem to not work as hard as you do. Additionally, you may be confused when hard work does not lead to recognition, such as a promotion.

Beliefs affect your interaction with others. For instance, you could have a belief that people are good. This could lead you to first assume positive intentions about another person's actions. If they do something you do not agree with, you are more likely to pause and think about their motivations as being well-intended, rather ill-intended.

Most of the time, you do not even think about why you do what you do. But every now and then, life throws a curveball that forces you to stop and think. Imagine believing in total honesty, only to find yourself in a situation where telling the whole truth might hurt someone you love. Moments like these make you dig a little deeper into your belief system.

BELIEF IN ACTION

Do you remember the first time you rode a bicycle? The belief that you could keep your balance helped lead to success, while doubt often ended in a fall. This foundational concept applies to more complex parts of our lives, too. Think back to that exhilarating feeling when you finally pedaled a bike without falling. Was it magic? No, it was *belief in action*. Just as you trusted the wheels and your own balance, you have a set of core beliefs navigating you through the winding roads of life.

Remember the scrapes and bruises from those falls off the bike? Those were not failures. They were simply part of the learning process. Similarly, your beliefs may have led you down some unexpected paths, and you may have encountered setbacks. Perhaps you went to law school with the goal of working at a large firm, only to discover that your dream job wasn't what you expected. This is where real learning and growth occur.

Now, imagine that bike ride again, but as an adult. Do you worry that when you get on a bike you will fall? No, you now think more about where you are going, how fast you are going, your safety, and other more adult-like thoughts. You are not merely trying to keep your balance. You are navigating toward a destination. For example, if you are thinking of going back to school, you think about the personal, professional, and financial layers of the decision, not just about the advantages of the new knowledge and degree.

Your beliefs are like handlebars, guiding you through obstacles, helping you make the right turns, and leading you toward your goals. Understanding them equips you with tools to design your future with conscious intention.

Kristen, a former chief marketing officer, took her belief to the next level. "There was this heart-stopping moment when I chose to leave my secure, high-level job at a Fortune 40 company," she says. "After thirty years, climbing from a part-time clerk to a PR executive, I made a daring leap of faith." Kristen credits a deep, personal belief in herself for providing the courage to make such a bold move. "This belief wasn't just about success," she says. "It was about self-respect and following my heart. Starting my own company was scary, but it felt incredibly right."

Similarly, Lindsay, a senior leader of operational transformation, used her belief in herself to make a bold job change. "I decided on the spot to leave a professional environment that was unhealthy without a safety net to catch me," she says. "I put my career and personal life on the line. I believed that I am resourceful enough to tap into my abilities and know exactly how to use them to build myself back up from nothing and reimagine my future, one day at a time."

THE DUAL NATURE OF BELIEFS

Recognizing your beliefs and understanding their origin is a step in assessing whether they serve you well or hinder your progress. The good news? You are in control. Your beliefs are not set in stone. Once you identify them, you can change, revise, shape, and mold them to better fit who you are and what you want in life. Some beliefs empower and motivate you.

When rooted in positivity and self-assurance, beliefs can function as catalysts, propelling you toward your goals and helping you navigate challenges with resilience.

They can serve as a push to reach new heights and be open to new opportunities.

Positive beliefs about yourself can increase performance, motivation, and success. If you believe you can, you are already halfway there. If you see yourself as capable and strong, you set yourself up for success that leads to greater confidence and a stronger belief in your own capabilities.

Research on what is called the *growth mindset* pioneered by renowned psychologist Carol Dweck illustrates the impact of positive beliefs. According to her findings and subsequent research, people who embrace a growth mindset, believing that abilities can be developed through dedication and hard work, are more likely to persevere in the face of challenges and achieve their goals.

In contrast, negative beliefs can hinder your growth. A *fixed mindset*, the belief that abilities are static and unchangeable, hinders progress and leads to self-doubt. This mindset acts like a barrier, blocking the path to your potential.

Self-doubt, fear, or misconceptions can also act as barriers, holding you back from making changes and achieving what you want. Negative self-belief can cloud your vision, making it difficult to see opportunities or solutions right in front of you. In essence, while positive beliefs can be great allies, negative ones can be formidable obstacles. The power of belief is immense, and recognizing its impact is an initial step in harnessing it to your bold advantage. Let's look at examples of how some common limiting beliefs can create barriers.

IMPOSTER SYNDROME

Imposter syndrome is not just self-doubt. It is a deep-rooted belief a person holds that, despite evidence of their capabilities, they are a fraud. Karla, a project manager, often felt like a fraud when she presented in front of groups, particularly if the group included people she didn't know or C-suite executives. To her, presentations were more than slides and figures. They were a referendum on her professional worth, and she often believed that she didn't measure up. Karla's imposter syndrome convinced her that despite her accomplishments, she was merely wearing a mask of competence. People who have imposter syndrome struggle with reconciling self-perception and external accomplishment.

PERFECTIONISM

A belief that things must be perfect makes every new challenge not an opportunity but a potential point of failure. For example, Diana, a very experienced business-development leader, was asked to spearhead a new division to explore emerging markets. However, Diana was a perfectionist, and she fixated on the uncertainties and risks of not doing a good enough job. Her belief that her actions had to be flawless meant that the new venture wasn't just a career decision, but a battle against an ingrained need to always perform at the absolute highest level. Diana was poised on the cusp of an innovative venture, yet she was holding herself back.

RISK AVERSION

Everyday life comes with plenty of uncertainties, but some people are so afraid of risk that they play it safe despite being unhappy. For instance, Jennifer had decades of expertise in corporate finance. Throughout her career, she had played it safe, avoided risk, and was promoted. She had a significant interest in human resources and wondered if she could combine the skill sets in a new role. Her belief that her skills could be transferable and that she needed a change conflicted with her belief that she needed a stable career to support her family. Jennifer's risk aversion stood in the way of pursuing a career change that would have been more fulfilling. Her belief in career stability had served her well, so taking a gamble was way outside her comfort zone.

In each of these stories, belief is not just a backdrop, it is the protagonist, influencing decisions, shaping perspectives, and determining paths. As you read this book, I encourage you to observe and challenge what you believe and why. I don't suggest you should tear your beliefs apart. However, questioning beliefs that shape your life and may be holding you back gives you the power to learn, adapt, and thrive.

IDENTIFY YOUR CORE BELIEFS

Core beliefs are a subset of your beliefs. By delving into them, understanding their origins, and assessing their impact, you gain awareness that can help you better guide your life in directions that fulfill and inspire you. Core beliefs' distinction lies primarily in the depth, influence, and foundational role they play in your life. Let's take a look at how they differ from more general beliefs.

Core Beliefs

- **Foundational:** Core beliefs are deeply ingrained and fundamental to your understanding of yourself and the world. They are the central principles that shape your perspective on everything around you.

- **Influential:** Core beliefs significantly influence your thoughts, feelings, and behaviors. Core beliefs often operate at a subconscious level, guiding your decisions and actions in a profound way.

- **Formed early:** Core beliefs typically form in early childhood. Family, culture, individual experiences, and significant life events influence their development.

- **Resistant to change:** Because your core beliefs are so deeply seated, they are often resistant to change, even in the face of contradictory evidence.

Beliefs

- **Varied in depth:** Regular beliefs can range from superficial to more deeply held convictions, but they do not necessarily define your identity or worldview.

- **More flexible:** These beliefs are more amenable to change as you gain new experiences, information, and perspectives.

- **Contextual and specific:** Regular beliefs can be about specific, isolated concepts or ideas and may not be central to your identity or decision-making processes.

- **Less influence on behavior:** While general beliefs influence behavior and attitudes, they are usually less pervasive and less automatic than core beliefs.

Later in this chapter, you will draw a map of your core beliefs. Identifying your core beliefs is not merely a philosophical exercise. It is an analytical process of dissecting your thoughts, feelings, and actions to uncover the hidden convictions steering your life. It is a bit like a life audit. By recognizing where these beliefs come from, you can better evaluate their impact. When you identify a core belief, ask yourself: *Where did this belief come from? Is it helping me or holding me back?* The answers just might lead you to a happier, more fulfilled, and more aligned life.

YOUR BELIEFS AND YOUR VALUES

Let's take a look at how your beliefs relate to your values. Your *values* are the principles and beliefs that define what matters most to you in life.

Your values serve as the solid ground upon which you build your decisions, actions, and relationships.

There are connections between your values and your beliefs that are important to understand as you define your personal bold path. Key areas include the following:

Values

- Values are the principles or standards of behavior that you deem important in life. They are the fundamental convictions that guide and motivate attitudes and actions.

- Values reflect what is important to you, influencing priorities and serving as a benchmark for evaluating actions and decisions.

- Examples of values include honesty, integrity, compassion, respect, and responsibility.

Beliefs

- A belief is a firm, unyielding faith or confidence in yourself, your ideas, or a vision for the future. A belief is the conviction that something exists or is true.

- Beliefs are often based on cultural, familial, and societal norms and may be influenced by factors such as individual experiences, education, and religion.

- Examples include the belief that hard work will be rewarded, that you are capable of accomplishing your goals, and that people are fundamentally good.

HOW BELIEFS AND VALUES INTERCONNECT

Beliefs form the foundation upon which values are built. Your beliefs influence what you value, and these values guide your actions and decisions. Understanding the relationship between beliefs and values helps you comprehend why you behave the way you do.

- **Guiding principles:** Both beliefs and values serve as guiding principles in your life. While values dictate what you consider important, beliefs fundamentally shape how you perceive the world.

- **Influence on behavior:** Your beliefs influence your values. In turn, your values affect your actions. For example, if you value family based on a belief that family relationships are important to personal happiness, this value will influence how you interact with family members.

- **Determine your priorities:** You hold values that reflect your deepest beliefs about what is good, desirable, and worthwhile. These values influence how you set priorities.

- **Cultural and societal influence:** Cultural and societal context often shape beliefs. Beliefs, in turn, influence the values you adopt.

- **Personal identity and integrity:** Your beliefs and values contribute significantly to your personal identity. They help you define who you are and what you stand for, guiding you to live with integrity, according to your principles.

- **Decision-making:** Values guide your decisions, but values are often rooted in your deeper beliefs. For instance, a decision to pursue a career in social work may stem from a value of service to others, which is based on a belief in the importance of helping the less fortunate.

COMMON VALUES

While the list of values is extensive and diverse, here are some common ones:

- **Integrity:** The clear commitment to honesty, ethics, and moral principles. People with integrity are steadfast in upholding their values even in the face of challenges.

- **Creativity:** The drive to innovate, explore new ideas, and think outside the box. Creative people often find surprising solutions to complex problems.

- **Empathy:** The capacity to understand and share the feelings of others. Empathetic people foster a sense of belonging and mutual support in groups.

- **Resilience:** The ability to bounce back from adversity. Resilient people persevere in the face of setbacks.

- **Courage:** The willingness to take calculated risks and confront fear or uncertainty. Courageous people push themselves to step out of their comfort zones.

There is no hierarchy or judgment when it comes to values. Your unique combination of values makes you who you are. Embracing and honoring these values empowers you to live and lead authentically, making decisions and taking actions that resonate with your deepest convictions and unlock your limitless potential.

Dedicating time to reflect on your values is like hitting the pause button, allowing you to take a deep breath and peer into the heart of what truly matters. When you reflect on your values, you engage in a profound act of self-discovery. You uncover the principles that are nonnegotiable to you, the beliefs that shape your worldview, and the qualities that you hold dear. This introspection can be transformative, helping you gain clarity about your priorities, both personally and professionally.

ACTIVITY
ALIGN YOUR VALUES AND GOALS

This activity will help you explore your core values and how they align with your current goals. It helps you ensure that your actions and decisions are in harmony with what you truly value, leading to more fulfilling personal and professional outcomes.

1. LIST YOUR TOP FIVE VALUES

Choose five values that are currently your highest priorities.

2. DEFINE YOUR VALUES

For each value listed, write a brief definition of what it means to you, why it is important to you, and how it has influenced you.

3. LIST YOUR TOP FIVE GOALS

Choose five goals that are currently your highest priorities. They can be personal or professional and can range from short-term objectives to long-term aspirations.

4. ALIGN YOUR VALUES WITH YOUR GOALS

For each goal, write down which of your values align with it and how the value supports the goal. For example, if one of your goals is to lead a successful team, the value of empathy might be crucial in managing team dynamics.

5. REFLECT ON THE ALIGNMENT BETWEEN YOUR VALUES AND YOUR GOALS

Are there any discrepancies or areas where your goals don't fully reflect your values? Do any of your goals need to be adjusted to better align with your values? Conversely, are there values you need to focus on more to achieve your goals?

6. MAKE AN ACTION PLAN

Create an action plan for one of your top five goals that you believe would benefit from fine-tuning its alignment with your values. For instance, if creativity is a core value, your action plan might include setting aside time each week for creative thinking or projects. (You can do this for multiple goals, but pick one to get started.)

7. REVIEW REGULARLY AND ADAPT

Commit to regularly, for example, monthly or quarterly, reviewing your goals and values alignment and adjust as needed.

CORE BELIEFS AND CHOICE

Have you ever felt like you are stuck in a rut or treading water? It could be an old belief holding you back. For example, you want to exercise more, eat better, and feel healthier, but you believe you have no time to do these things. This is an example of a belief choosing for you because you are the person who controls your time and schedule. You are making a choice not to do these things. Instead, do you scroll for thirty minutes a day, when you could be walking, biking, or doing a workout?

Once you have identified your core beliefs and assessed which ones are serving you (and which ones are not), you have something incredibly powerful: your choice. You can choose to challenge the beliefs that hinder your growth or happiness, replacing them with ones that better align with your goals. You are the driver, the navigator, and the passenger all in one, and you get to decide where you want to go.

Lindsay, the senior leader of operational transformation from earlier in the chapter, used the review of her beliefs in The BOLD Framework to understand her actions. "The moment I understood that my decisions are shaped by my unconscious beliefs, I decided to go deep into learning the patterns and experiences that had me stuck in a mindset that kept recreating what I didn't want in life," she says. "Learning about myself, my childhood, and the coping mechanisms that I adopted gave me a platform to reframe how to move forward in life as a functional adult and become fully responsible for my destiny."

THE MAGIC OF "I BELIEVE"

The simple yet potent phrase "I believe" is a declaration, a commitment, and a powerful tool for change that you already have inside you. When you say, "I believe in myself," you are not merely expressing a thought. You are planting a seed of self-assurance, courage, and resilience. You are defining who you are and what you stand for. And from that solid ground, you can leap into action, knowing that your belief system is there to support and guide you. Consider the power of the following statements:

- **I believe I belong.** Believing you belong is a powerful assertion of self-worth that can lead to success in challenging environments. For example, you may be a woman in a field where women have been historically underrepresented. Your belief that you belong means recognizing your abilities and asserting your place without reservation. By standing strong and confident, you can establish your presence, even when surrounded by people who may not initially accept your role or authority.

- **I believe in following my passion.** Passion is a driving force behind creativity, innovation, and fulfillment. When you believe in pursuing what excites you, you're aligning yourself with opportunities that not only bring joy but also often lead to success.

- **I believe I am worthy.** Believing in your inherent worth means recognizing your value as a person. In a world obsessed with output and efficiency, it's crucial to remember that you are more than the sum of what you produce.

- **I believe I can succeed in new areas.** This belief focuses on transferable skills, adaptability, and the willingness to learn, which can open doors to exciting opportunities.

- **I believe in being intentional with my actions.** When you believe in the importance of being intentional, you can more easily make choices that resonate with your deeper beliefs and values.

- **I believe in eureka moments.** Flashes of insight can happen to anyone. Embracing your aha moments can help lead you to an unexpected and fulfilling journey.

"I BELIEVE" IN PRACTICE
The phrase "I believe" is more powerful than you might think. It is like a switch that can turn on confidence and motivation. It can give you a boost or hold you back. When you say it with conviction, it is like giving yourself a pep talk and a green light to boldly pursue your goals and dreams. On the flip side, if you say it half-heartedly or laced with doubts, it can feel like you have one foot on the brakes. Consider the following examples of helpful and hindering "I believe" statements.

Examples of Helpful "I Believe" Statements

- I believe in my ability to overcome challenges.
- I believe every setback is a setup for a greater comeback.
- I believe in my unique talents.
- I believe kindness and empathy make the world a better place.
- I believe in my dreams and my power to make them a reality.
- I believe every day offers a new opportunity to learn and grow.
- I believe in the strength of my convictions and standing up for what's right.
- I believe perseverance and dedication will lead to success.
- I believe in the goodness of people and the value of genuine connections.
- I believe with a positive mindset, anything is possible.

Examples of Hindering "I Believe" Statements

- I believe I'm not good enough, no matter how hard I try.
- I believe others have it easier than I do.
- I believe I'm destined to fail, regardless of my efforts.
- I believe I don't have what it takes to succeed.
- I believe people don't truly value or appreciate me.
- I believe my mistakes define who I am.
- I believe opportunities are for others, not for someone like me.
- I believe I'm always at a disadvantage.
- I believe my dreams are unrealistic and out of reach.
- I believe I don't deserve happiness and success.

Think about some "I believe" statements that support your dreams and desires to move forward and make changes. Write them down. During the week, reread them for inspiration.

"Boldness shines brightest when beliefs are challenged."

ACTIVITY

DRAW YOUR BELIEF MAP

In this activity, you will draw a map of your core beliefs. Belief mapping is an introspective practice used to visualize the beliefs influencing various areas of your life. It can help you identify and reinforce positive beliefs, or address and reframe limiting ones. Below are questions that can help you explore personal, professional, health, and mindset beliefs.

Grab paper or your journal and a pen and find a peaceful corner where you can reflect. As you work through this exercise, be open and honest.

1. IDENTIFY YOUR CORE BELIEFS

- Start with the basics. What are some of the fundamental beliefs that guide your daily decisions and long-term goals? (See step 4 for some questions to get you started.)
- Write them down as they come to mind. Don't worry about making them sound profound. They may be positive or negative—don't judge them.
- Pick out three to six beliefs to explore in more detail. (Example: "I believe in being kind to everyone, even those who are unkind to me.")

2. ASSESS THEIR ORIGINS

- Time to play detective. Where did these beliefs come from? Was it from parents, teachers, friends, or personal experiences? Understanding their roots can provide insight into why you hold them so closely.
- Write down some of your thoughts. (Example: "My belief in kindness was instilled in me by my grandmother, who always treated people with respect.")

3. ANALYZE THEIR INFLUENCE

▶ Now, look at your beliefs like a friend giving you advice. Are they helping you grow, like the belief in hard work, or are they acting as roadblocks, like a lack of confidence in public speaking?

▶ Try to see the real impact they have on your life. (Example: "My belief in hard work has driven me to achieve my career goals, but my fear of public speaking has hindered my professional growth.")

4. CREATE A PLAN FOR CHANGE

▶ If you find beliefs that are keeping you from being your best self, consider how you can modify or replace them. Maybe a public speaking course can help you overcome your fear, or a conversation with a mentor might reshape a limiting belief.

▶ Try to remodel your belief system to make it more "you." (Example: "I will attend a public speaking workshop to build my confidence and redefine my belief about my speaking abilities.")

Here are some questions to consider as you draw your belief map:

Personal Beliefs

▶ What beliefs do you hold about yourself and your potential?

▶ How do your beliefs influence your personal relationships?

▶ What do you believe about your ability to find joy and fulfillment in hobbies or activities?

▶ What are your beliefs regarding learning and personal growth?

▶ Do you have beliefs about your place in the world or your ability to effect change?

Professional Beliefs

- What are your underlying beliefs about work and success?
- How do you perceive your skills and value in a professional setting?
- What do you believe about the nature of competition and collaboration at work?
- What beliefs do you hold about the trajectory of your career or professional development?
- How do you view your network and professional relationships?

Health Beliefs

- What are your core beliefs about health and wellness?
- How do you perceive your body's strengths and limitations?
- What beliefs influence your dietary and exercise habits?
- How do your beliefs affect your approach to mental health and self-care?
- Do you hold any beliefs that may be preventing you from achieving your health goals?

Mindset Beliefs

- What do you believe about the power of a positive or negative mindset?
- How do your beliefs dictate your response to stress and adversity?
- What do you believe about learning from failure and success?
- How strong is your belief in your ability to adapt and grow?
- What do you believe about resilience and bouncing back from setbacks?

TRANSFORM YOUR BELIEFS

Mapping your core beliefs can identify those that are helpful and aligned with your authentic self, and those that are holding you back. As you reshape your beliefs, these guidelines can support you:

- **Be patient.** Reshaping your beliefs is not an instant process. It's a continuous journey, filled with self-reflection and growth. Be bold in your pursuit, but gentle with yourself along the way.

- **Reach out for help.** If you're uncertain, reach out to those who know you best. Friends, family, colleagues, or mentors can provide valuable insights. Often, a fresh perspective is the missing key to clarity.

- **Note milestones.** Your journey will be paved with successes, failures, and realizations. Acknowledge them. Make friends with them. Invite them in for a coffee or just sit with them. Be proud of these moments, which are milestones on your bold journey.

- **Navigate with integrity.** Remember that this journey is not about tearing yourself down or erasing your existing beliefs. The goal is to hone and align your beliefs to resonate with who you truly are today.

KEY TAKEAWAYS

Your beliefs are your life's road map. They are the silent force steering your decisions, shaping your behaviors, and setting the tone for the roads you choose to travel.

Beliefs impact every action and decision. From what you say to yourself in the mirror each morning to the choices you make in your relationships and career, your beliefs are always there, guiding the way.

The power of positive and negative beliefs is real. Encouraging beliefs can move you forward, while doubts can act like brakes on your dreams.

Values are part of the equation to bold action. Your personal values serve as a foundation for boldness. Values like integrity, authenticity, and determination drive bold behaviors and decision-making, enabling you to face challenges confidently and live in alignment with your true self.

Boldness upholds your values. Being bold often means standing firm in your beliefs and values, even when faced with opposition or uncertainty, and being true to your values in everyday life.

WHAT'S NEXT

The next chapter tackles belief conflict, a situation where your established beliefs, especially core ones, confront new information or opposing viewpoints. You will explore how belief conflicts are not just challenges but also opportunities for personal growth. You will move from mapping your beliefs to navigating the conflicts that arise between them, offering valuable insight into your bold journey and how change can energize your progress forward.

BOLD MEANS

"Not being afraid and not holding back, particularly when it's something you believe in."

—Julia Boorstin, senior media and tech correspondent for CNBC and author of *When Women Lead*

On *The Bold Lounge* Podcast

CHAPTER 5

CONQUER BELIEF CONFLICT

"Where beliefs clash, boldness brings clarity."

In The BOLD Framework, *believe* is the first foundational step in implementing change in your life. You have explored how your beliefs influence what you do and how you see the world. They can push you forward or hold you back. But what happens when your beliefs collide with each other?

Belief conflict influences how you perceive and interact with the world, and more importantly, how you make decisions and take action. Beliefs are not just passive thoughts. They actively shape your reality. Picture a crossroads where two potent beliefs pull you in different directions. These intersections can be challenging, but they're also opportunities for profound growth and self-discovery.

In this chapter, you will look at what happens when your beliefs don't align with your actions, how your body and mind react to belief conflict, and why resolving belief conflict matters so much as you move forward on your bold path. Remember those myths we debunked in chapter 3? They may show up as you wrestle with some of your belief conflicts in this part of the journey.

CAUSES OF BELIEF CONFLICT

Your beliefs act as the lens through which you view the world. They influence your perceptions, attitudes, and behaviors. When your beliefs are in harmony, your actions and decisions align seamlessly with your values. However, when conflicts between beliefs arise, they can lead to discomfort, indecision, and inconsistent actions. For example, belief conflicts can lead to hesitation, inconsistency, and even paralysis in decision-making. Unresolved belief conflicts can negatively affect your well-being, relationships, and professional success. By understanding the roots and recognizing the signs of belief conflicts, you can develop strategies to resolve them and realign your beliefs, paving the way for a more coherent and authentic life experience.

Root causes of belief conflict include:

Cognitive dissonance: Cognitive dissonance, a term coined by psychologist Leon Festinger, occurs when you hold contradictory beliefs, or when your beliefs are at odds with your actions or decisions. For example, you may believe that exercise is important to your health, but not incorporate it into your life by prioritizing your schedule to make time for it. This dissonance creates psychological tension that you are motivated to resolve. Cognitive dissonance can inspire you to change your beliefs or behaviors to restore internal harmony.

Societal and cultural influences: Beliefs are significantly influenced by societal norms, prevalent ideologies, conventions, and your cultural background. Societal and cultural influences can lead to internal conflicts, especially when your personal beliefs clash with widely accepted expectations. Prevailing norms can also conflict with each other. For example, women often face contradictory messages in terms of working and being a parent.

Personal experiences and upbringing: Your personal history, including upbringing, education, and life experiences, shapes your belief system. Early life experiences, family dynamics, and significant life events all contribute to the development of your beliefs. Sometimes, these ingrained beliefs may conflict with new perspectives you encounter later in life, leading to belief conflicts.

COMMON BELIEF CONFLICTS
Here are common belief conflicts, including several that are specific to women. Do you relate to any of these examples?

External Belief Conflicts
These conflicts highlight the challenges that arise when personal desires bump up against external societal pressures.

- **Career vs. family:** Pursuing a career versus dedicating time to family responsibilities, often influenced by societal expectations around parenthood, particularly for mothers
- **Independence vs. cultural expectations:** Valuing personal autonomy and making choices for yourself versus adhering to rigid norms and expectations
- **Traditional femininity vs. modern empowerment:** Traditional notions of femininity versus the modern empowerment movement that encourages women to break barriers
- **Beauty standards vs. self-acceptance:** Conforming to societal beauty standards vs. embracing and celebrating your natural appearance
- **Singlehood vs. partnership:** Cherishing independence as a single woman versus feeling the societal pressure or personal desire to find a partner or marry
- **Parenthood by choice vs. societal pressure:** Deciding whether or not to have children based on personal choice versus societal expectations
- **Compassionate vs. authoritative leadership style:** Being compassionate and nurturing versus assertively exerting authority
- **Public image vs. private authenticity:** Maintaining a public image, often influenced by societal expectations, versus being authentic to yourself in private spaces
- **Workplace equality vs. traditional roles:** Advocating for equal opportunities and treatment in the workplace versus navigating environments that might still uphold traditional gender roles
- **Self-care vs. caretaking:** Taking time for self-care versus being the caretaker for others, whether it's children, partners, or aging parents

Internal Belief Conflicts
These conflicts highlight the challenges that arise when two (or more) internal beliefs seem to contradict each other.

- **Moral vs. practical:** When your moral or ethical beliefs clash with practical or pragmatic considerations—for example, believing in environmental conservation but finding it challenging to give up certain conveniences that harm the environment

- **Ideal self vs. real self:** Struggling between who you want to be (ideal self) and who you actually are (real self)—for instance, aspiring to be altruistic and generous, yet not finding the time or money to support charity

- **Short-term desires vs. long-term goals:** The battle between immediate gratification and long-term aspirations—for example, the desire to indulge in unhealthy foods versus the goal to maintain a healthy lifestyle

- **Belief vs. action:** When personal beliefs are not reflected in actions—for example, believing in honesty but finding yourself occasionally bending the truth to spare someone hurt feelings

- **Conflicting personal values:** Holding two important values that sometimes oppose each other—for example, valuing both career advancement and family time, yet finding these two in conflict when allocating your time

- **Personal belief vs. cultural belief:** When personal beliefs clash with those traditionally held by your culture or family in areas such as relationships, career choices, or lifestyle—for example, choosing to become a single parent

- **Risk aversion vs. aspiration for change:** The internal conflict between the desire to avoid risk and the aspiration to make significant changes in your life—for example, wanting to start a new business but being afraid of financial insecurity

- **Independence vs. need for approval:** Struggling between the desire to make independent choices and the need for approval or validation from others—for example, choosing a career path that others might consider impractical

- **Intellectual beliefs vs. emotional responses:** Experiencing a conflict between what you know intellectually to be true or right and emotional responses that suggest otherwise—for example, feeling unworthy or incapable despite knowing intellectually that you have the necessary skills

- **Future self vs. present self:** Conflict between what is beneficial for your future self and what the present self wants or feels—for example, saving money for future security versus spending it for immediate pleasure

HOW TO IDENTIFY BELIEF CONFLICTS

Identifying belief conflict involves recognizing the signs of internal conflict between your beliefs and actions, which include:

- **Emotional discomfort:** Often, the first sign of belief conflict is a feeling of unease or discomfort. For example, you find yourself feeling unexpectedly anxious, guilty, or uncomfortable about a decision and are unsure why.

- **Inconsistencies in beliefs and actions:** Pay attention to situations where your actions do not align with your stated beliefs. For example, you value and desire personal time but find yourself constantly checking your work email.

- **Rationalization or justification:** If you frequently find yourself rationalizing or justifying your actions or beliefs, especially when your reasoning stretches logic or contradicts previous statements, it may be due to a belief conflict.

- **Avoidance behavior:** Sometimes, people avoid information or situations that might highlight or exacerbate conflict between their beliefs and actions. If you notice a pattern of avoidance in certain areas, it is worth exploring.

- **Conflicting thoughts:** Notice whether you often have thoughts or decisions that contradict each other, especially about important topics.

- **Seeking confirmation:** If you constantly seek reassurance or validation for a particular belief, it could be because it conflicts with another deeply held belief.

- **Intense reactions to opposing views:** Strong emotional reactions to opinions or facts that contradict your beliefs may be a sign of an underlying conflict.

- **Mental fatigue:** Ongoing belief conflicts can lead to mental exhaustion because your mind is constantly trying to reconcile the conflicting beliefs or justify your actions.

To identify belief conflicts, it is crucial to practice self-reflection and mindfulness. Being honest with yourself about your beliefs and motivations can help you uncover areas of cognitive dissonance.

ACTIVITY
WHAT ARE YOUR BELIEF CONFLICTS?

To identify your belief conflicts, ask yourself the following reflective prompts. Write down your observations.

▶ Do my actions align with my beliefs?

▶ How do I feel when my actions contradict my beliefs? Do I feel discomfort, guilt, or unease, for example?

▶ Am I frequently justifying or rationalizing my actions to myself or others to explain away behavior that doesn't align with my beliefs?

▶ Are there situations, topics, people, or information I avoid because they challenge my beliefs?

▶ What are my emotional reactions to opposing viewpoints? Do I feel defensive, angry, or upset, for example?

▶ Do I feel internally conflicted about important decisions?

▶ Are there areas in my life where I feel consistent discomfort or unease?

▶ How do my beliefs about myself align with my self-esteem and self-image?

▶ Am I seeking external validation for actions or beliefs I'm unsure about?

▶ Do I experience mental fatigue or stress when thinking about certain aspects of my life due to the effort of reconciling conflicting beliefs?

"In the face of conflicting beliefs, be boldly curious."

DECIPHER THE WARNING SIGNS

At the heart of many belief conflicts are deep-seated beliefs that do not serve your current ambitions. Sometimes, these are remnants from past experiences, societal expectations, or family teachings that no longer align with who you are now or aim to become. Regularly questioning and challenging your internal narratives can help unveil these hidden barriers, opening the door for change and growth.

Noticing the early signs of belief conflicts allows for timely course correction. Your body and mind often signal when your beliefs are not in sync with your actions. You may experience some of the following symptoms.

EMOTIONAL SYMPTOMS

As mentioned above, you might feel persistently unsatisfied, restless, or even guilty without an evident reason. These feelings linger, creating an underlying sense of discontent. You might experience recurring negative thought patterns, heightened self-doubt, or a persistent feeling of being "stuck." If you often feel regret or unease after making decisions, it's worth considering whether those choices truly resonated with your beliefs.

PHYSICAL SYMPTOMS

Your body has a way of sounding the alarm when your spirit is not at peace. Chronic stress from belief conflicts can manifest in various physical ways: sleep disturbances, unexplained aches, or even frequent illness. Belief conflicts can drain your physical energy, making it mentally harder to focus and make decisions.

SOCIAL SYMPTOMS

The mental and physical fatigue caused by belief conflicts can make it harder to interact with others. Relationships might suffer as you struggle to articulate the source of your unrest, leading to misunderstandings or conflicts. When living in a state of incongruence, simple tasks can seem daunting, and previously enjoyable activities might lose their charm.

BEHAVIORAL CHANGES

You might notice yourself procrastinating more or putting off specific tasks. Examples of avoidance behaviors include sleeping more, bingeing on social media or online entertainment, or increased drinking.

When you recognize what could be signs of belief conflicts, try not to panic or judge yourself. These red flags are not inherent flaws, but rather feedback mechanisms that invite you to pause, reflect, and recalibrate. Ignoring these signs can compound misalignment, leading to deeper feelings of detachment or even depression. By acknowledging these signals, you gain information that will help you identify their underlying causes. For example, is it a particular aspect of your job that is clashing with a personal belief?

Wendy, a cyber security expert, believed in the value of hard work and was dedicated to her job. However, her job was incredibly stressful, which conflicted with her belief in self-care. "I was working in a very toxic environment with women who were very unsupportive of me, because I was an outsider coming in," she says. "I was so stressed all the time. No matter what I did, it was wrong. One day, I said, enough." She quit even though she didn't have a new job lined up. "I knew I was good at my job, and I had plenty of other people who believed in me," Wendy says. "I just needed to believe in myself and, most importantly, take care of myself."

To identify belief conflicts, sometimes an external perspective can be enlightening. Trusted friends, family, or mentors can often see what you might be blind to. They can point out patterns or behaviors that do not seem like "you" or where you've unknowingly veered off course. Engaging in open conversations where you share your feelings, doubts, and aspirations can help you gain clarity. However, it's essential to ensure that this feedback doesn't dictate your path but rather serves as another tool for self-awareness and realignment.

Once you pinpoint the causes, you can take actionable steps, which the next chapter covers, to resolve the conflicts and realign your beliefs. This could mean making subtle shifts or a larger life change.

THE BENEFITS OF ALIGNED BELIEFS

Your life is a unique journey, filled with its own set of challenges and choices. One key element that helps you navigate this journey is ensuring that your beliefs and actions are in harmony by resolving belief conflicts. This alignment impacts everything from your personal happiness to overall success.

Here are some benefits of aligned beliefs:

Peace in a busy life: Modern life often requires juggling various roles and responsibilities. When your actions reflect your true beliefs, you can feel a sense of inner harmony, even during busy or stressful times. This alignment acts like an anchor, providing stability and peace of mind.

Confident decision-making: Life is full of decisions, and making these choices can sometimes be overwhelming. However, when you are clear about your beliefs, decision-making becomes more straightforward.

Authentic living: Authenticity is the ability to be true to yourself, not about adhering to external expectations. When your actions align with your beliefs, it is easier to live authentically and experience a genuine sense of fulfillment.

Meaningful relationships: Aligned beliefs can help strengthen relationships.

Resilience in the face of adversity: Aligned beliefs give you a solid foundation to rely on during tough times. This congruence between belief and action provides strength and resilience, enabling you to face and overcome obstacles more effectively.

Continuous learning: Aligned beliefs foster a mindset open to growth and learning. In fact, continuous learning is so integral to your bold journey that it's the third foundational step of The BOLD Framework, which part 4 covers.

In essence, aligning beliefs with actions creates a life that is meaningful. It is a journey of self-discovery and empowerment, where each step you take is in harmony with your beliefs. Living by your aligned beliefs carves out a clear path forward for you to live authentically.

The journey to alignment is not a onetime event but a continuous process. There will be moments of doubt, challenges, and deviations. The warning signs you encounter when you have belief conflicts are not setbacks but rather guiding lights to illuminate your path, not obstruct it. Instead of dreading these signals, embrace them. Each time you course-correct, you refine your journey, making it more authentic and fulfilling.

"To change a belief is to unlock a door you did not know existed."

KEY TAKEAWAYS

Belief conflict occurs when you hold contradictory beliefs or ideas simultaneously. Recognizing and addressing these internal conflicts is crucial within The BOLD Framework because beliefs influence perceptions, decisions, and actions.

Belief conflicts stem from root causes. Causes include cognitive dissonance, societal and cultural influences, and personal experiences.

Your body and mind will signal to you when you have belief conflicts. Emotional, physical, social, and behavioral symptoms and changes may result from a belief conflict. These feedback mechanisms are an invitation to reflect on belief conflicts, identify their root causes, and move forward to resolve them.

When your beliefs are aligned, your actions and decisions are consistent with your beliefs. This alignment leads to a more coherent and authentic life experience.

WHAT'S NEXT

Awareness of belief conflicts is merely the start of resolving them. Recognizing that you have veered off course is vital, but it is what you do next that truly defines your journey. In the next chapter, you will dig into the power of reframing your beliefs, crafting a life where your beliefs and actions align with your bold purpose.

BOLD MEANS

"Bold is a proactive choice. It's about making a choice when you don't have to do something that feels out of your comfort zone."

—Dorie Clark, Columbia Business School professor, *Wall Street Journal* bestselling author, and three-time Top 50 business thinker named by Thinkers50

On *The Bold Lounge* Podcast

CHAPTER 6
REFRAME YOUR BELIEFS

"Each reframed belief is a ripple, capable of creating waves of profound change."

In the last chapter, you identified your belief conflicts, which happen when you have multiple beliefs competing against each other. This results in misalignment between what you believe and what you do. In this chapter, the final one focused on the first foundational step of The BOLD Framework, *believe*, you will learn how to resolve these conflicts through the art of reframing your beliefs and aligning them with your actions.

Belief reframing is the process of challenging and changing limiting or negative beliefs to more positive and empowering ones. Reframing is not about discarding your beliefs, but about recognizing, understanding, and adjusting them to better serve your goals and aspirations. In The BOLD Framework, this process will solidify your foundation of belief, which will then support you as you transition to the next foundational phase: *own*, covered in part 3.

You will also define what success means to you, which will give you additional insight during belief conflicts. From societal norms to workplace standards, there's a constant stream of conflicting ideas about what success "should" look like and the pressure to meet the expectations that go along with them. By defining success on your own terms, you can steer your life and career with intention, while simultaneously inspiring those around you to seek their own authentic paths.

Since the first chapter, you have been practicing listening to your inner voice and thinking about making a bold change. Maybe it is the urge to stretch beyond your current boundaries, elevate what you already have, or align your actions more closely with your beliefs. Now, firmly grounded in your beliefs, you are moving closer to your goal of change.

HOW TO REFRAME YOUR BELIEFS

In your journey of personal growth, you will encounter belief conflicts, as you learned about in chapter 5, that can hinder your progress and well-being. These conflicts, arising from your deeply held yet contradictory beliefs, can create significant stress and impede your ability to be bold and effect change in your life.

However, by mastering the art of reframing, you can transform these conflicts into beliefs that support and empower you, reshaping your perceptions and attitudes to foster a more positive and productive mindset. When beliefs are in harmony with your aspirations, they act as powerful catalysts, propelling you forward with renewed purpose and vigor.

Let's explore how to reframe belief conflicts, using a step-by-step approach with a practical example, to turn challenges into opportunities for growth and self-improvement.

REFRAMING PROCESS

Belief conflict example: "I must always achieve perfection in my work, but this often leads to stress and disappointment when I fall short. This conflicts with my belief that I am capable of doing a good job."

To reframe a belief, follow these steps:

1. **Identify the negative belief.** Recognize the belief causing conflict—the need for perfection and the resulting stress and disappointment.

2. **Challenge the belief.** Question the validity and helpfulness of this belief. Ask yourself: *Is it really true that I must be perfect? Is it possible for anyone to always achieve perfection? What are the consequences of holding on to this belief?*

3. **Consider a more balanced perspective.** Look for evidence that contradicts the belief or indicates that it might not be entirely accurate. For example, recall times when you did well without being perfect, or when learning from mistakes led to better outcomes.

4. **Develop a new, supportive belief.** Create a belief that acknowledges the effort and progress rather than just the outcome. For instance, "Striving for excellence is important, but perfection is not always achievable. My worth is not solely dependent on achieving perfection. Learning and growing from each experience is more valuable than being perfect."

5. **Reinforce the new belief.** Look for opportunities to reinforce this new perspective in your daily life. When you find yourself striving for perfection, remind yourself of your new belief. Recognize and celebrate the effort and improvement, not just the flawless result.

By reframing the belief, the focus shifts from a negative, perfectionist viewpoint to a more supportive and growth-oriented perspective. Here's how the example of being a perfectionist might play out in real life: You complete a project at work and notice some minor errors. Your immediate thought is, "I've failed to make it perfect. This is not good enough." After going through the reframing process, you gain a new perspective. Now your thought might be, "While there are some errors, I've put in a significant effort, and the overall project is strong. These mistakes are opportunities for learning and improvement next time. My value comes from the effort and progress I've made." This change in mindset can reduce stress and increase satisfaction and resilience.

REFRAMING STRATEGIES

As you practice reframing beliefs, the following strategies may help:

Increase your awareness. The previous chapter focused on how you can identify belief conflicts in your life. That time was well spent because that increased awareness will take you far in resolving conflicts when they occur in specific contexts. For instance, if tensions exist between your work and home responsibilities, it will be easier to recognize when they happen. So, instead of having a vague sense of unease, you can name the conflict and even plan strategies in advance to prevent and address it if needed. For example, you can set boundaries like Amira, who chose not to check her work email on the weekends and to leave the office at the same time every day.

Imagine your future self. Picturing yourself in a future where newly embraced beliefs are fully integrated can be powerful. For instance, Sonia, a new director, struggled with the belief that she lacked the experience of other successful business leaders and was not sure how to network. She envisioned confidently meeting other leaders at events and having more assuredness in her own expertise. This vivid mental image became a source of inspiration, pushing her to seek more opportunities to meet others.

Engage in a *belief swap*. These are collaborative discussions where people share beliefs and, as a collective, offer alternative, empowering perspectives. When Zoe, a junior architect, expressed her belief that her designs were too unconventional for clients, a senior colleague recounted how the world's most iconic structures once faced similar skepticism. This external input helped Zoe see her unique designs not as hindrances, but as potential future landmarks based on swapping her belief with the one her colleague shared.

Seek feedback. Seeking feedback from others provides new perspectives and insights that may challenge your existing beliefs and open the door to alternative ways of thinking. This external input can be instrumental in breaking down rigid thought patterns and fostering a more flexible and supportive mindset. Olivia, a tech lead, believed she wasn't tech-savvy enough for innovative projects. Regular feedback sessions with her team revealed that they admired her not just for her technology skills, but also for her ability to bridge the gap between complex tech jargon and practical applications, a niche she had not recognized.

Accept that you cannot entirely avoid belief conflict. Along your bold journey, you are going to reframe beliefs, especially those that are not accurate or helpful. But there will always be some give and take with beliefs when it comes to real life. Just like you can feel multiple emotions at the same time, you can have equally strong beliefs that will butt up against each other. For example, if you seek more alignment between work and home, you are bound to encounter dilemmas with equally good and bad choices. At these times, use your deeper understanding of your beliefs to make the choice that is right for you in the moment, knowing that you can continue to revisit the topic.

Through such deliberate and varied approaches, the process of reframing beliefs becomes dynamic and impactful, enabling you to align more closely with your goals.

HARNESS THE POWER OF ALIGNED BELIEFS

Clarity can sometimes seem elusive. Yet, one of the most transformative steps you can take is aligning your beliefs with your actions and your dreams. This alignment serves as a guide, cutting through the noise and illuminating what truly matters to you. Instead of being constantly swayed by external pressures or fleeting trends, you can find a steady compass in your genuine beliefs. This clarity will guide your decisions and shape your future, acting as a catalyst for meaningful change.

When you sync your beliefs with your daily actions, you are likely to begin to eliminate activities, habits, and sometimes even relationships that no longer serve your true self. In their place, you will find or create opportunities that resonate deeply with your beliefs. When your actions reflect your authentic self, this congruence invites increased fulfillment and joy.

When your life choices and actions echo your true beliefs, the ceiling of your potential begins to rise. No longer held back by self-doubt, societal expectations, or conflicting beliefs, you may embrace challenges with renewed excitement and energy. You may take risks that were previously intimidating, explore avenues you had once overlooked, and open doors you didn't even know existed. This alignment doesn't just benefit you. Its ripple effects touch everyone around you. When you operate from a place of authenticity, you inspire others to do the same. Your decisions, driven by aligned beliefs, often lead to more meaningful interactions, stronger relationships, and lasting impacts on your communities.

HOW REFRAMING YOUR BELIEFS SUPPORTS YOUR SUCCESS

Belief reframing can be transformative. Here are five key benefits of this powerful mental shift.

- **Enhanced self-esteem and confidence:** Reframing beliefs around self-doubt into positive affirmations can boost your self-worth. This renewed confidence can lead to a more proactive approach to challenges and opportunities.

- **Improved mental health:** Negative beliefs can contribute to stress, anxiety, and depression. By reframing these beliefs, you can reduce negative emotional responses, promoting overall mental well-being and resilience.

- **Increased motivation and drive:** Replacing beliefs that hinder progress with those that promote growth can ignite motivation. When you believe you can achieve your goals, you are more likely to take action and persevere through setbacks.

- **Better decision-making:** Belief reframing can lead to clearer thinking by removing cognitive biases or self-imposed barriers. This clarity can result in more informed and objective decision-making.

- **Strengthened relationships:** By reframing beliefs about yourself and others, you can foster healthier communication, understanding, and empathy in your relationships. Letting go of preconceived notions or judgments can pave the way for deeper connections and mutual respect.

"Belief reframing isn't just thought alteration. It is a revolution of your inner self."

HOW YOUR BELIEFS DEFINE SUCCESS

Beliefs play a pivotal role in shaping your understanding of success. Your beliefs serve as filters through which you perceive the world and your place within it. When your actions are in harmony with your beliefs, you experience alignment and satisfaction. Conversely, when there's a disconnect or a belief conflict, feelings of discontent and unease can arise, even if you're achieving external markers of success. That's because societal expectations, professional milestones, and external validations often color how success is perceived.

Every success is not posted for the world to see. You can have quiet successes that no one needs to see, but you are still succeeding, nonetheless. The most potent and fulfilling definition of success is deeply personal and supports your core beliefs. Continuously examining and, if necessary, realigning your beliefs ensures that your definition of success encompasses not just external achievements but also internal harmony and fulfillment.

For example, take Barbara, a seasoned project manager, whose success extended beyond keeping projects on task and on time. Her signature strength was growing and developing each of her team members, a talent anchored by her core belief that everyone can learn. It was most clearly on display in moments like when a junior analyst stepped up to handle a critical client meeting or when her team brainstormed innovative solutions. To her, these were the indicators of true success.

On the other hand, for Rebecca, a finance director, success meant maintaining a work-life alignment, supporting her work team, and contributing to the community. It was not only about hitting financial and profitability milestones but also attending her child's sports events, taking evenings off to rejuvenate, volunteering for school events, and sitting on the board of the local food bank.

Like Barbara and Rebecca, defining your version of success reflects your individual aspirations, values, and priorities. And in that uniqueness lies its true power. When you define success for yourself, which you'll do in the following activity, it becomes a driving force, a beacon guiding you with clarity and purpose, irrespective of the noise around you.

"Write your own success story, one that resonates with your heart."

ACTIVITY
DEFINE WHAT SUCCESS MEANS TO YOU

Defining success is a deeply personal endeavor, and it's essential to reflect on what truly matters to you.

This activity will help you develop a personal definition of success, one that aligns with your deepest values, aspirations, and sense of self. By answering the following questions, you will gain clarity on what success means to you beyond conventional metrics. Set aside some quiet time for reflection and write down your thoughts for each prompt.

1. WHAT BELIEFS MATTER MOST TO YOU?

- Reflect deeply on the beliefs that shape your life. Consider experiences where these beliefs were highlighted.

- Write about moments when adhering to these beliefs brought you satisfaction or a sense of accomplishment.

- Ask yourself, *How do these beliefs influence my career choices, relationships, and personal goals?*

2. HOW DO YOU WANT TO FEEL DAILY?

- Envision your ideal day. What emotions are most present? Is it a sense of peace, the thrill of challenges, the joy of creativity, or the stability of routine?

- Think about times when you've felt these emotions and what triggered them. This can give clues to the activities or environments that align with your version of success.

3. WHAT LEGACY DO YOU WANT TO LEAVE BEHIND?

- Contemplate the mark you want to leave on the world. This could be through your profession, personal activities, or interactions with others, for example.

- Write a brief legacy statement that encapsulates the impact you wish to have. Consider how your daily actions contribute to this legacy.

4. WHAT ACHIEVEMENTS WOULD MAKE YOU PROUD?

- List specific achievements that would bring you a sense of pride. These could range from professional milestones to personal growth victories.

- For each achievement, explore why it's important to you. This understanding can help prioritize your efforts and goals.

5. HOW DO YOU DEFINE ALIGNMENT IN YOUR LIFE?

- Think about what alignment or balance means to you. How would you ideally divide your time and energy among work, relationships, personal interests, and self-care, for example?

- Consider times when you felt out of alignment. What was missing or overwhelming? Reflecting on these experiences can help you identify the components of what a well-aligned life looks like to you.

As you answer these questions, look for themes or recurring ideas. These will be key indicators of your unique definition of success. Your answers may evolve over time. Revisit these questions periodically to see how your thoughts and life circumstances have changed and how these changes have influenced your definition of success.

A PERSONALIZED BLUEPRINT FOR SUCCESS

Dedicated time for self-reflection is key to creating a personalized blueprint for what success looks like to you. Consider the milestones and moments in your life that have brought genuine satisfaction. Did they include leading a high-stakes project to completion, mentoring a junior team member, or participating in a well-executed collaborative effort? Volunteering, watching your kids play soccer, or having a date night with your partner? Analyzing these instances can offer clues to what success genuinely looks like for you.

Establishing clear boundaries is also crucial. Recognizing areas you are unwilling to compromise on, be it work-life alignment, self-care, ethical considerations, or personal growth paths, provides additional information for your blueprint of success. These boundaries ensure that as you take your bold journey, you remain true to your core beliefs.

Also, I encourage you to remain adaptable as life changes. The business landscape, personal aspirations, and external factors evolve. Regularly revisiting and refining your goals, which you'll do in the next activity, ensures they remain relevant and aligned with your actions. Success is not merely reaching your goals but also ensuring your journey resonates with purpose, passion, and authenticity.

"In the alignment of goals and beliefs, there lies the harmony of purpose and action."

ACTIVITY
REFINE YOUR GOALS

To ensure that your goals have depth, are rooted in genuine passion, and are truly aligned with your beliefs, practice the "What Will This Give Me?" technique. For every goal, ask, "What will this give me?" four times. After answering the question four times, end with asking yourself how this is connected to why your specific goal is important. Understanding your *why* can motivate you to take action and persist in accomplishing your goal.

HERE'S AN EXAMPLE:

What is my goal?
I want to become the CEO.

▶ What will this give me?
The ability to influence big decisions in my field.

▶ And what will this give me?
The ability to effect changes I believe need to be made.

▶ And what will this give me?
The ability to share my innovative ideas.

▶ And what will this give me?
The ability to revolutionize the field.

▶ So, why is this goal important?
I want to serve others and make a difference, which is a core belief for me.

Now try it for yourself. Write down your answers on the next page.

What is my goal?

↓

What will this give me?

↓

And what will this give me?

↓

And what will this give me?

↓

And what will this give me?

↓

So, why is this goal important?

UNLOCK NEW HORIZONS THROUGH ALIGNED BELIEFS

When you reframe and realign your beliefs, you open doors to a world of new opportunities. Your beliefs are lenses through which you view the world, and when those lenses are cleaned and polished to align with your true self, you gain a clearer, more focused perspective. In essence, the journey of aligning your beliefs and actions unlocks a version of your life rich in purpose, potential, and profound joy.

Imagine every day being a step closer to your authentic self, where every bold choice you make and every action you take feels just right. Sure, there might be moments of doubt, but these are opportunities to refine and revise your approach and learn from the journey. In a world full of countless directions and pressures, bold clarity emerges when you align your beliefs with your actions and aspirations.

KEY TAKEAWAYS

Belief reframing is transforming limiting or negative beliefs into positive, empowering ones. This practice is not about discarding your beliefs but realigning them to better serve your aspirations and goals, fostering growth and self-fulfillment.

Define success on your own terms. For a definition of success that resonates deeply with your true self, align it with your core beliefs.

Authenticity involves aligning your beliefs with your actions. Being authentic and aligned in your beliefs frees up energy you can use toward actions that bring you closer to your goals.

WHAT'S NEXT

The next section focuses on the second foundational element of The BOLD Framework: *own*. This step is about acting intentionally and moving forward with a disciplined approach as you forge your own path to success. Think of it as the part where you roll up your sleeves and get down to business. Determination will be your driving force and passion your fuel to keep moving forward.

PART 3

OWN

Dive into the second foundational step of The BOLD Framework: *own*. You will craft a Wheel of Ownership and chart your course to greater agency and confidence. As a result, you'll deliberately take control of your actions, decisions, and, ultimately, your destiny, ensuring that your external realities align with your internal convictions.

BOLD MEANS

"Having the confidence to dream big, unwieldy dreams and finding the strength to take action on them, particularly when they run contrary to what is expected of you."

—Candace Nelson, founder and bestselling author of *Sweet Success: A Simple Recipe to Turn your Passion into Profit*, and Guest Shark

On *The Bold Lounge* Podcast

CHAPTER 7

INTENTIONAL AND PURPOSEFUL OWNERSHIP

"To own your life is to own every decision and every consequence that comes with it."

You have now reached the second foundational step of The BOLD Framework: *own*. In exploring the first foundational step—*believe*—you uncovered the transformative power of reframing beliefs and confronting the internal stories that can constrain your potential. But to ignite real transformation and action, you will now step into the pivotal realm of ownership—embracing your actions and their outcomes, both the triumphs and the trials, with full responsibility.

The journey to defining personal ownership begins with a deep dive into self-reflection. Think back to times when you were profoundly in sync with your actions. For example, I recall, early in my career, steering a project that was riddled with obstacles. Many saw it as a sinking ship. Yet, every choice I made and every risk I embraced was a testament to my unwavering belief in its success. When it did succeed, it wasn't just a professional victory; it was also a powerful affirmation of my dedication and conviction to owning the outcome. Instances like these, where your efforts and their outcomes are deeply intertwined, shine a light on the essence of true ownership.

OWNERSHIP, ACCOUNTABILITY, RESPONSIBILITY, AND AGENCY

Let's begin by distinguishing between four concepts related to this step: ownership, accountability, responsibility, and agency. While they're connected, each one has a unique meaning. They also share similarities and differences.

Definitions

- **Ownership:** This is the act of recognizing and accepting personal control over or possession of your actions and decisions. Here, you claim something as your own, whether it's an idea, a task, or a tangible item. Imagine you are playing a game of basketball. Ownership is like claiming the ball as yours.

- **Accountability:** This is the willingness to answer for your actions and decisions, good or bad. It means standing up and saying, "I did this," and then facing the consequences, whatever they may be. In basketball, accountability is stepping up whether you make or miss a shot.

- **Responsibility:** This refers to having an obligation to complete specific tasks or uphold certain standards. Being responsible means you are entrusted with something and expected to handle it appropriately. In basketball, responsibility is carrying out your role's assigned tasks to the best of your ability.

- **Agency:** This is the capacity to act independently and make your own choices, free from external forces and based on others' core beliefs and values. In basketball, agency is how you choose to carry out your role, such as to shoot or pass.

Similarities

- **Ownership vs. accountability:** Ownership is more about claiming and accepting that something, such as an action, is yours. Accountability is about answering for the results of that action, regardless of whether it leads to success or failure.

- **Ownership vs. responsibility:** Ownership is about claiming something as your own. Responsibility is about the obligation associated with that thing. For example, you might own a car, but you have a responsibility to maintain it and drive it safely.

- **Accountability vs. responsibility:** Accountability is about answering for outcomes. Responsibility is about the duties you have. You're accountable for the results of those duties. For instance, if you are responsible for a project at work, you will be held accountable for its success or failure.

- **Agency vs. the rest:** Agency stands out from the other three concepts because it is about the power to make choices based on free will. While ownership, accountability, and responsibility are closely related to actions, decisions, and outcomes, agency is about the inherent ability to make those decisions in the first place.

Differences

- At their core, these concepts intertwine around actions and decisions. Ownership, accountability, and responsibility are like three pillars supporting the structure of your actions.
  - You claim it (ownership).
  - You have a duty toward it (responsibility).
  - You answer for it (accountability).
- Agency, on the other hand, is the foundation upon which these pillars stand. It is the power and autonomy that allow you to erect these pillars in the first place. While the first three concepts are about the what and how of actions, agency is about the why and your inherent freedom to choose.

"Being bold means being your authentic self in all aspects of your life. Personally and professionally. Privately and publicly. Stepping into your light and fully embracing everything that makes you, you."
—Melissa Hurrington, CFO and VP of operations at Premier Claims

THE ESSENCE OF OWNERSHIP

Ownership is about taking responsibility for your actions, decisions, and outcomes. It is the conscious choice to step forward, claim your space, and recognize that you hold the power to shape your destiny. While this concept is universally applicable, for women, understanding and embracing ownership is especially pivotal.

Historically, women have often been relegated to the background, their voices muted and their contributions overlooked. In such a context, passive acceptance can become the default. With more women breaking barriers and shattering glass ceilings, the importance of ownership has become more pronounced. When you take ownership, you assert your worth and capability and challenge stereotypes and biases that have possibly held you back. This act of ownership sends a powerful message: You are not just a participant but also a leader in your own right, steering your bold journey with confidence and conviction.

Ownership extends beyond personal growth. It becomes an example for others that can inspire and empower them to step up, be bold, and act with purpose. When you embody ownership, you amplify your voice and the voices of others who look up to you. This ripple effect can have a transformative impact. Ownership unlocks potential, challenges norms, and paves the way for lasting change. By taking ownership, you not only elevate yourself but also set the stage for future generations to thrive, lead, and succeed.

ACTIVITY
OWNERSHIP IN ACTION

Think of a time when you took complete ownership of a situation, be it in your personal or professional life. How did this ownership manifest in your actions and decisions? Write down your thoughts.

OWNERSHIP AND BOLDNESS: A SYMBIOTIC RELATIONSHIP

In a world where change is constant, the boldness to adapt, innovate, and evolve is essential. But this boldness is anchored in ownership. When you own your roles, responsibilities, and outcomes, you are more inclined to make bold decisions because you understand the weight of your actions and are prepared to stand by them, come what may.

Revisit your personal definition of boldness from chapter 2. When paired with boldness, ownership transforms into a powerful force, pushing boundaries, challenging norms, and driving impactful change in yourself and others. I associate boldness with the audacity to step out of my comfort zone, take risks, and venture into the unknown. Our definitions of boldness may differ, but being bold can often involve making decisions that might be unpopular, facing challenges head-on, and standing firm when you encounter adversity.

For example, Kristen, now chief executive officer, took a courageous stand when she encountered injustice in her former role. "The day I stood up against the unfairness and gender discrimination at work was the day I truly owned my path," she says. "It was terrifying, knowing I might lose friends and respect at the company I'd loved for so long. But this decision to speak out, even to the CEO, was mine. It was about being true to myself. Leaving to start my own venture was my stand—a statement that I deserved better."

To be truly bold, you must own your actions and decisions. This means celebrating successes, accepting failure, and learning from both. Ownership without the spark of boldness can lead to stagnation. Conversely, bold moves without a sense of ownership can result in directionless steps. It is the combination of the two that creates a road map for visionary change and groundbreaking innovation. The combination also fosters resilience. When faced with setbacks or challenges, if you embrace both boldness and ownership, you are more likely to persevere, adapt, and overcome—and learn, grow, and reaffirm your commitment to change.

THE POWER OF OWNERSHIP
Ownership is not just about accepting responsibility. It's also about embracing the power you have over your life and your future. Success is often a direct reflection of this sense of ownership. By taking charge of your actions, accepting responsibility, and being proactive, you set the stage for achieving your dreams and goals.

Key benefits of ownership include:
- **Increased accountability:** When you take ownership of your actions and decisions, you're more likely to hold yourself accountable for the outcomes. This heightened sense of responsibility leads to more

thoughtful decision-making and a proactive approach to problem-solving.

- **Enhanced motivation and commitment:** Ownership fosters a deep sense of personal investment. When you feel that a project or goal is "yours," you're more motivated to put in the effort and perseverance required to see it through to success.

- **Empowerment and confidence:** Taking ownership empowers you to take control of your personal and professional life. It builds confidence as you recognize your ability to influence outcomes and navigate challenges effectively.

- **Clarity of purpose:** Ownership helps clarify your purpose and align your actions with your beliefs and goals. When you own your path, you are more likely to set goals that are meaningful to you and pursue them with purpose and determination.

- **Personal and professional growth:** Ownership is a powerful driver of growth. It encourages you to step out of your comfort zone, take on new challenges, learn from your experiences, and continuously develop your skills and knowledge.

- **Better problem-solving skills:** With ownership comes the need to tackle obstacles head-on. This proactivity fosters improved problem-solving skills because you are more invested in finding effective and innovative solutions.

- **Increased respect and recognition:** Taking ownership can lead to increased respect from others. People are more likely to trust and respect someone who demonstrates a strong sense of ownership.

- **Long-term success and fulfillment:** Ultimately, taking ownership of your actions and decisions leads to long-term success and fulfillment. It aligns your daily activities with your larger life goals.

OWNERSHIP STARTS WITH YOU

Ownership is a deeply personal connection to your actions, your choices, and their subsequent outcomes. The decisions you make directly reflect your values, beliefs, and intentions, but you cannot genuinely take pride in something or fully accept responsibility for it unless you truly own it.

Taking pride in something goes beyond just feeling good when things go right. It is also understanding the effort, intention, and dedication that went into achieving that outcome. When you launch a successful project, the pride you feel isn't just because of the positive results. It's also because you know the meticulous planning, the sleepless nights, and the relentless determination that went into making it a success. Similarly, when things don't go as planned, true ownership means accepting the setback, understanding the reasons, and using the experience as part of a learning curve. Pride lacks substance if it is not accompanied by genuine ownership.

Intentionality in action (which we'll discuss in more detail in chapter 14) is another facet of ownership. Without intentionality, actions lack clarity and focus. When you act with intention, you are not reacting to situations or external pressures. Instead, you are proactively shaping your path. And to ensure that this path is authentic and true to who you are, you must own every step you take, every decision you make. Intentionality emphasizes the proactive and deliberate aspect of ownership, purposefully directing your actions toward a desired goal or change.

Thus, taking ownership is not just about being responsible for outcomes (reactive), but also about consciously shaping those outcomes (proactive). This distinction can be particularly empowering because it encourages you to accept responsibility for your actions and actively engage in shaping your path.

At its core, ownership is a commitment to yourself. It's a pledge to stay true to who you are, uphold your beliefs, and relentlessly pursue what you want to achieve. It's not about control in the traditional sense, where you seek to dominate or dictate terms. Instead, it is about having control over your choices and actions. While you might not have control over external events, you always have control over how you respond to them.

For example, Lindsay, the operational transformation leader from chapter 4, took ownership when she applied to graduate school. "I decided to own my career and get myself into graduate school, even though English was my second language," she says. "My spouse at the time did not support my decision to get further education, and I had a full-time job and a three-year-old recently diagnosed with special needs. None of that stopped me from pursuing going back to school because I knew, as an immigrant, that it was the only way to opt into a better future and opportunities for myself and my son."

OWNERSHIP ON THE MAIN STAGE

Here's an example of ownership in action. Rita, an expert in the fashion industry, was challenged by unhelpful team dynamics in the department she led that resulted in low morale. Rather than imposing top-down solutions, she initiated open dialogue sessions, inviting everyone to share their perspectives, including views on how she could improve. This inclusive approach, born out of her sense of ownership for her role and her team, transformed the department's work ethos to be much more positive. Rita's sense of ownership was multifaceted, encompassing her responsibility for the team dynamics, work environment, team empowerment, proactive problem-solving, and her accountability as a leader. Let's look at each in turn.

- **Team dynamics:** Rita recognized that the team's unhelpful dynamics and low morale were issues that, as a leader, she needed to address. She didn't shy away or pass the responsibility to others but took it upon herself to initiate change.

- **Work environment:** Her decision to engage in open dialogue sessions demonstrated her ownership of the overall work environment and culture within her department. She understood that as a leader, she influenced the atmosphere and team ethos.

- **Team empowerment:** By choosing an inclusive approach that invited everyone to share their perspectives, Rita owned her role in empowering her team. She acknowledged that part of her responsibility was to ensure that team members felt heard and valued.

- **Proactive problem-solving:** Instead of resorting to authoritative or prescriptive solutions, Rita chose to actively engage by fostering communication. She took ownership of finding a sustainable and collaborative solution.

- **Accountability as a leader:** Rita understood that the performance and morale of her team were, in part, reflections of her leadership style and actions. By addressing these problems head-on, she embodied a sense of accountability for her team's success and well-being.

ACTIVITY
DEFINE OWNERSHIP

This activity will help you define and internalize the concept of ownership in a way that resonates personally and professionally. You will explore how to tailor the broad concept of ownership to your unique life circumstances and learn to identify the moments that require your ownership. The process will give you a clearer, more personalized understanding of what ownership means to you and equip you with practical strategies to assert ownership, leading to more intentional and impactful actions.

1. REFLECT ON EXAMPLES OF OWNERSHIP

▶ Write down instances in your life where you felt a strong sense of ownership over your actions and decisions. These could be in professional settings, personal projects, or even daily tasks.

▶ Write down how these instances made you feel and the outcomes they produced.

2. DEFINE OWNERSHIP

▶ Reflect on your beliefs and values and how your sense of ownership aligns with your actions and decisions.

▶ Write your personal definition of ownership.

3. CONSIDER OWNERSHIP SCENARIOS

▶ Imagine or recall specific scenarios where the need for ownership was unclear. For each scenario, ask yourself:
  - Did this situation align with my core beliefs?
  - Could my involvement have made a meaningful impact?
  - What held me back from taking ownership if I didn't?

▶ Write down any insights on what motivates your sense of ownership.

4. REFLECT AND ADJUST

▶ Regularly reflect on your ownership experiences. Consider noting in a journal instances where you successfully implemented your ownership and areas for improvement.

WHEN TO HOLD OWNERSHIP

Now with a personal definition of ownership in hand, your next challenge is application. When do you step up, and when do you step back? The nature of the task or decision often holds the answer. If it is an area where your expertise shines, then taking ownership makes sense. If it falls outside your domain, trusting someone with more knowledge in that area might be the wiser choice. Look to personal experiences and values to guide you on what to own and what not to own, knowing when to embrace and when to relinquish.

For example, while I felt confident leading operational initiatives, finance was not my strong suit. In one instance, instead of taking charge of a financial forecast, I entrusted it to a team member with a financial background. The results were not only more accurate but also provided fresh insights that I had not considered. If a project or decision evokes a deep emotional or intellectual connection, it can be a cue to take charge. However, continuously stepping in might stifle others' growth, especially if you are part of a team.

Another pivotal lesson I learned was during a new process launch I was leading. My inclination was to oversee every detail, given its significance. However, I recognized a team member's deep interest and innovative approach. By consciously stepping back and allowing her to take ownership, not only did the product launch succeed, but it also fostered an environment of trust and inclusion.

OWNERSHIP REFLECTION CHECKLIST

This activity provides an overview of where you are taking ownership in your life and where there may be room for improvement. It encourages self-awareness and sets the stage for actionable steps toward balanced ownership across different life areas. Regularly revisiting and updating your checklist can be a great way to track your growth over time.

1. PREPARE YOUR CHECKLIST

▷ Write down the following eight key life areas:
- Personal development
- Career/professional growth
- Personal relationships (family/friends)
- Financial management
- Health and well-being
- Learning and education
- Leisure and recreation
- Community involvement

2. REFLECT AND INVENTORY

▷ For each life area listed, take a moment to reflect on your recent actions and decisions in that area. Ask yourself the following questions to guide your reflection:
- Have I made deliberate decisions in this area recently?
- Do I feel actively involved and responsible for the outcomes in this area?
- Am I making choices that align with my values and goals?

▷ Based on your reflections, decide whether you are taking ownership in that particular area.

- If you feel you are actively and intentionally engaged, making choices that reflect your values and working toward your goals, put a check mark (✓) next to that area.

- Be honest with yourself during this process. It's okay if not all areas have a check mark. The goal is to gain a true picture of where you stand in terms of personal ownership across different aspects of your life and highlight areas for potential growth.

- If you're unsure about a particular area, think about the last time you felt a sense of achievement or fulfillment in that area. This can often be a good indicator of ownership.

3. ASSESS AND PLAN

- Look at the areas you've checked. Acknowledge your efforts in taking ownership there.

- For unchecked areas, consider why you may not be taking ownership. Is it due to lack of interest, resources, or time? Note these reasons.

- Set one or two simple goals for one of the unchecked areas where you want to improve your ownership.

The moment you step off the sidelines, stop waiting for circumstances to magically align, and instead take the reins, owning your decisions and actions and moving forward with boldness and unshakable conviction, the world transforms in unimaginable ways. This is the power of ownership, the gateway to a world where you're not just a participant, but an active creator of your destiny.

"In owning your flaws and strengths, you find the true power of boldness."

KEY TAKEAWAYS

True transformation requires actively owning your decisions and actions. Ownership is crucial for genuine and sustainable forward motion on your bold journey.

Craft a personal definition of ownership. Through introspection and reflection on experiences where your efforts directly influenced outcomes, you can define ownership to align with your core beliefs.

Ownership enables you to assert your worth and capability. Ownership also enables you to take charge when you choose to, steer your journey with confidence, challenge stereotypes, and inspire others.

When paired with boldness, ownership is a powerful force for driving change. Boldness requires owning your actions and decisions, which includes accepting both successes and failures.

Ownership has many benefits. These include increased accountability, motivation, empowerment, clarity of purpose, personal and professional growth, improved problem-solving skills, respect, and long-term success.

WHAT'S NEXT

The evolution of ownership is empowerment, which the next chapter covers. Empowerment is a catalyst that urges you forward, arming you with the confidence and tools to seize ownership and make impactful decisions. In professional contexts, empowerment manifests as the support and resources that enable you to rise to challenges, grow, and innovate. On a personal level, empowerment is the strength to make choices that resonate with your true self, the courage to voice your opinions, and the resilience to navigate life's challenges.

"Doing something that scares you a little, but that you believe to be in support of your purpose or growth—and accepting the real possibility of failure."

—Amy Edmondson, professor at Harvard Business School and author of *The Fearless Organization* and *Right Kind of Wrong*

On *The Bold Lounge* Podcast

CHAPTER 8
OWNERSHIP FUELS EMPOWERMENT

"Every owned choice is a step toward empowerment."

The second foundational step in The BOLD Framework is *own*. In the previous chapter, you explored the concept of ownership, wrote a personal definition, and looked at how you can implement ownership in daily life. When you truly own your choices and actions, you feel a unique kind of power: empowerment.

Think of empowerment as your inner powerhouse, fueling your journey with drive and confidence. It is more than a fleeting sense of achievement. It is a deep-rooted belief in your capabilities and a commitment to rise above challenges with grace and strength. This chapter is about igniting the fire of empowerment within you. You will uncover the transformative synergy between taking ownership and feeling empowered, which will start you on your bold path with renewed vigor and vision. Get ready to discover how you can act and truly feel that power from within.

"Boldness is the courage to be different in a sea of sameness. Own your uniqueness and let it shine brightly."

Ownership is like driving a car. You decide where to go, how fast, and when to stop. Sometimes, you might take a wrong turn or face a roadblock. But when you own your journey, you learn, persevere, and find a way forward.

Once you have a firm grip on that steering wheel, something magical happens: You begin to feel more empowered. Empowerment means knowing you have the ability to shape your destiny—you can tackle any challenge, learn from any mistake, and continuously grow and evolve. In real life, be it in school, sports, relationships, business, or career, the principle remains the same. When you own your choices and actions, you set the stage for genuine empowerment, progress, and success. You make a conscious choice to be in charge, to not let external factors or self-imposed barriers dictate your path. Let's unpack how to take the next steps.

THE FOUR CORE COMPONENTS OF EMPOWERMENT

Empowerment is a profound transformation that encompasses self-awareness, confidence, autonomy, and competence. By delving into each of these core components, you can better appreciate their significance in shaping how empowerment can have a lasting impact in various spheres of your life.

SELF-AWARENESS: A MIRROR TO YOUR PASSION

At the foundation of empowerment lies *self-awareness*: the ability to introspectively evaluate yourself, recognizing strengths, understanding weaknesses, acknowledging core beliefs and values, and tapping into your passions. For women, this is especially significant in a society that often imposes historically gender-based expectations and stereotypes.

Real-life example: Born in Pakistan, Malala Yousafzai recognized her passion for education and the value she placed on it, especially in the face of cultural opposition. She is the youngest Nobel Peace Prize laureate. Despite facing life-threatening challenges, her acute self-awareness enabled her to champion the cause of girls' education globally. Her journey underscores the power of knowing your convictions and acting upon them.

CONFIDENCE: THE INNER FLAME

Confidence is an intrinsic belief in your abilities, ideas, and worth. For many women, cultivating confidence is challenging, especially when faced with societal or self-imposed doubts.

Real-life example: Oprah Winfrey's story is a testament to the power of confidence. Facing numerous adversities, including poverty, discrimination, and personal traumas, Oprah had a firm belief in herself and her vision, which led her to become a global media leader. Her confidence not only elevated her career but has also inspired countless women worldwide to believe in their unique potential.

AUTONOMY: YOUR INDEPENDENCE

Autonomy is the essence of self-governance. It underscores the significance of making independent decisions, free from external pressures. For women, asserting autonomy can be especially empowering in personal and professional realms, particularly when challenging traditional norms.

Real-life example: Indra Nooyi, the former CEO of PepsiCo, exemplifies the power of autonomy. As one of the few women leading a global corporation, Nooyi made bold, independent decisions that shaped the company's trajectory. Her autonomous leadership, often balancing global corporate demands with personal values, showcased how women can lead with distinction at the highest levels.

COMPETENCE: THE TOOL FOR CHALLENGES

Competence is about honing skills and abilities to navigate challenges effectively. It's the culmination of knowledge, experience, and continuous growth. Developing competence in a chosen area can lower your risk of engaging in negative self-talk and doubt.

Real-life example: Jane Goodall, the renowned primatologist, exemplifies competence. Although she initially lacked formal training, her passion for understanding chimpanzees led her to the forests of

Gombe. Her meticulous observations and groundbreaking discoveries showcased her unparalleled competence in primatology and challenged established scientific norms. Her journey underscores that competence, combined with passion, can revolutionize fields.

"The essence of empowerment lies in the courage to shape your own narrative."

Empowerment's core components—self-awareness, confidence, autonomy, and competence—are interconnected. Self-awareness and confidence are the internal pillars of empowerment. Self-awareness provides clarity about your strengths and values. Confidence is the force that drives you to act on this self-knowledge. Autonomy and competence are external manifestations of empowerment. Autonomy shows the world that you are a decision-maker who can chart your own path. Competence, meanwhile, is the tangible proof of your capabilities, the results of your experience and expertise.

Similarly, confidence is often built on competence. Knowing you excel in your field can boost your self-belief. True autonomy can only be exercised if you have the self-awareness to understand which decisions align with your core values.

ACTIVITY
HOW ARE YOU EMPOWERED TO SUCCEED?

Take a moment to reflect on your personal journey toward empowerment by answering the following questions. Write down your answers, which can provide valuable insights into your current state of empowerment and illuminate areas for further growth and exploration.

1. SELF-AWARENESS

- What are three strengths I bring to my personal and professional life?
- Which areas do I believe require growth or improvement? (List up to three.)
- What core beliefs drive my decisions and actions? (You can refer back to your answers from chapter 4's belief map activity.)

2. CONFIDENCE

- Can I recall a situation where my self-belief helped me achieve something I initially thought was out of reach?
- What internal or external factors sometimes shake my confidence?
- How can I reinforce my self-belief in the face of doubts or setbacks?

3. AUTONOMY

- In which areas of my life do I feel I have the most control? The least?
- Have I ever made a decision that went against the norm because it aligned with my personal beliefs or values? How did it feel?
- What steps can I take to assert more independence in areas where I feel constrained?

4. COMPETENCE

- What three skills or knowledge areas am I most proud of?
- Are there new skills I'm keen to acquire or existing ones I'd like to hone? (List up to three.)
- How can I ensure continuous learning and growth in my personal and professional endeavors?

THE ROLE OF EXTERNAL FACTORS IN EMPOWERMENT

Empowerment is not just an inward journey. The world around you, the people you engage with, and the societal structures you are part of significantly influence your path to empowerment. These external factors shape, support, and sometimes challenge your empowerment. Recognizing and leveraging supportive communities, drawing inspiration from mentors and role models, and actively challenging societal barriers can significantly bolster your empowerment.

SUPPORTIVE COMMUNITIES

Communities offer more than just a sense of belonging. They can give you the boost you need to stay true to your beliefs and be bold. Whether it's a close-knit family, a connected group of professionals, or a community based on shared interests, these environments can be instrumental in bolstering your empowerment. A supportive community acts as a safety net, allowing you to take risks, express yourself, and grow. It provides a platform for shared experiences and mutual learning. For many women, these communities become spaces of validation and encouragement.

MENTORS AND ROLE MODELS

Mentors and role models can act as guides, inspiring and lighting the path to empowerment. Mentors, with their experience and wisdom, can help you navigate personal and professional challenges. They can provide feedback, share their experiences, and often open doors to opportunities. Role models, while they might be distant or even unapproachable, serve a different purpose. Their life stories, achievements, and even failures offer lessons and inspiration. They illustrate what's possible, challenging you to strive for more.

OVERCOMING SOCIETAL BARRIERS

Societal norms, expectations, and prejudices can act as barriers to empowerment. These invisible chains, often deeply embedded in culture and tradition, can limit your aspirations and potential. However, recognizing these barriers is the first step to dismantling them. This involves challenging age-old norms, questioning stereotypes, and sometimes swimming against the tide. When you challenge and overcome societal barriers, you empower yourself and pave the way for others to do the same.

STRATEGIES TO CULTIVATE EMPOWERMENT

Cultivating empowerment demands intention and consistent effort. Let's explore some strategies that can help you strengthen your sense of empowerment.

SET CLEAR GOALS AND WORK TOWARD THEM

Every journey begins with a destination in mind. In the context of empowerment, this destination translates to well-defined goals. Setting clear objectives provides direction, focus, and a sense of purpose. This clarity is especially crucial, given the myriad roles and responsibilities you most likely juggle.

Strategy in action: Begin by picking one short-term or long-term goal that embodies a bold change you want to make in your life. Write down the goal. Then list actionable steps needed to achieve it—keep the steps small and achievable. Set a deadline for the first step. Once you finish a step, set a deadline for the next, moving forward until you've reached your goal. This incremental approach makes the journey more manageable and provides consistent markers of progress. Celebrate achievements, big and small, along the way. They serve as affirmations of progress and encourage further motivation.

CONTINUOUSLY LEARN AND BE CURIOUS

Chapter 10 explores in detail the third foundational step in The BOLD Framework: *learn.* The world is dynamic. To remain empowered, effective, and relevant, continuous learning is essential. Being curious and learning is about growing and exploring the world.

Strategy in action: Allocate dedicated time for learning. Begin by picking one activity and putting time on your calendar to pursue it. You could watch a webinar, enroll in a course, or simply set aside time for reading. Diversify your learning by both deepening your current expertise and broadening your horizons. For instance, if you work in a tech role, consider exploring interpersonal communication or organizational psychology. Embracing a multidisciplinary approach through a lens of curiosity fosters a holistic sense of empowerment.

SEEK FEEDBACK AND BE OPEN TO GROWTH

Feedback, when approached constructively, is a gold mine for promoting growth. It can provide insights into your areas of strength and help you pinpoint where you'd like to make changes.

Strategy in action: Contribute to building an open feedback culture within groups you're a part of, such as your work team, organization, family, or friends, that supports both giving and receiving feedback. When soliciting feedback, be specific and avoid a generic "Do you have any feedback for me?" Instead, ask about a specific action, such as a recent report. Process feedback objectively.

To effectively seek feedback and be open to growth, here are some examples of questions you can ask yourself and others:

When Soliciting Feedback

- Can you provide specific examples of what I did well in my recent presentation?
- In what areas could I improve my performance on the last project?
- How do you think I handled the team meeting? What could I have done differently?
- What is one thing I could change to make my reports more effective?
- Regarding my recent interaction with the client, what are your thoughts on how it went?

When Reflecting on Feedback Received

- What is the key takeaway from the feedback I received?
- How does this feedback align with my personal and professional goals?
- What specific actions can I take to address areas of improvement?
- Which aspects of the feedback can I act on immediately? Which require long-term changes?

The key is not to take feedback personally but to view it as a tool for growth. Equally, when giving feedback, ensure that it's constructive and delivered empathetically.

BUILD RESILIENCE AND LEARN FROM SETBACKS

In your bold journey, setbacks are inevitable. Projects might not go as planned or even fail, decisions can misfire, and unexpected challenges can arise. Let's be real: Not everything you do can be a home run. You are going to have base hits, walks, and big-time strikeouts. However, empowerment isn't about the absence of failures or challenges. It's about resilience in the face of them. It's about bouncing back, learning from setbacks, and emerging stronger.

> *"I believe that when I fall, I'm building that muscle to being even bolder and more courageous."*
> —Ariel Belgrave Harris, an award-winning health and fitness coach, on *The Bold Lounge* Podcast

Adopt a growth mindset by viewing challenges as opportunities for learning rather than insurmountable hurdles. Step back and ask yourself, *What went wrong? What went right? What could I have done differently? How can this learning be applied in the future?* Journaling can be a valuable tool in this reflective process. Equally important is self-care. Building resilience requires emotional strength and physical well-being. Regular breaks, mindfulness practices, and exercise can bolster your resilience, equipping you to better navigate challenges with grace and efficacy.

KEY TAKEAWAYS

Claim ownership. Recognize that you are in control of your actions and decisions, and accept both your successes and your failures.

Feeling empowered is a result of taking ownership. Empowerment is the knowledge and belief in your ability to shape your destiny and tackle challenges.

Self-awareness, confidence, autonomy, and competence are the interconnected core components of empowerment. Self-awareness and confidence are internal aspects of empowerment, while autonomy and competence are external manifestations.

External factors can play a positive role in bolstering your empowerment. For example, supportive communities and mentors can help you thrive.

WHAT'S NEXT

The next chapter continues the second foundational step of The BOLD Framework: *own*. You will dive deeply into agency and confidence. Agency is your ability to make and own decisions. Confidence, a deep-seated belief in yourself, reflects your inner empowerment and is a manifestation of ownership. Agency and confidence are essential for succeeding on your bold journey, especially through challenges and opportunities. This duo empowers you to take charge of your actions and decisions, reinforcing your belief in your abilities. It is like wearing a badge that proclaims, "I believe in myself and am the architect of my life!"

BOLD MEANS

"Equal parts excited and scary . . . and you must do it to fulfill your purpose."

—Michelle Pecak, visionary supply chain executive and master connector

BOLD MEANS

"Doing what your gut tells you to do, what you feel is important and meaningful to you, and not worrying about what other people say."

—Liz Elting, founder and CEO of the Elizabeth Elting Foundation, and *Wall Street Journal* bestselling author of *Dream Big and Win: Translating Passion into Purpose and Creating a Billion-Dollar Business*

On *The Bold Lounge* Podcast

CHAPTER 9
AGENCY AND CONFIDENCE

"Confidence isn't just felt. It's built choice by choice, day by day."

The previous chapter discussed how intentional ownership leads to empowerment. This chapter focuses on agency and confidence, additional key elements of the second foundational step of The BOLD Framework: *own*. Having explored how owning your actions leads to empowerment, let's now explore how together ownership and the resulting empowerment enable you to exercise agency and build confidence in your life.

Think of your daily life as a series of choices. Small daily choices lay the groundwork for the larger, life-changing decisions. Understanding this helps you see the bigger picture—that both types of choices are important in crafting the story of your life. From the small decisions, like what to wear or what to eat, to the bigger ones, like where to live and what to do for work, each choice shapes your path.

Agency is your power to make these decisions, big and small, consciously and confidently. Think of agency as your personal navigation system, steering your life in the direction you choose on your bold journey. It is the mechanism that enables you to make decisions that are true to yourself. As we discussed in chapter 8, confidence is an intrinsic belief in your abilities, ideas, and worth. This chapter will guide you in recognizing your agency, showing you how to use it effectively to build confidence. Let's dive in and discover how you can harness these powerful tools to shape your journey toward a bolder, more confident you.

AGENCY, CONFIDENCE, AND BOLDNESS: WHAT'S THE DIFFERENCE?
This chart provides a deeper understanding of the similarities and differences between agency, confidence, and boldness.

Concept	Definition	Similarities	Differences
Agency	The ability to make choices and control your actions	Rooted in personal empowerment, drives decision-making	Focuses on decision-making, not necessarily outwardly visible
Confidence	Belief in yourself and your abilities	Rooted in personal empowerment, enhances decision-making	Derived from self-belief, can be perceived by others
Boldness	Courage to take risks and act innovatively; confidence in action	Drives action, influences decision-making	Involves risk-taking, more externally observable

To summarize:

- Agency is about making your own choices.
- Confidence comes from believing in yourself.
- Boldness includes having the courage to take risks.

"Small choices lead to big changes.
That is the power of agency in action."

AGENCY AND PERSONAL FREEDOM

Agency and personal freedom go hand in hand, and both play a role as you define and follow your bold path. Agency provides the capacity to make choices. Personal freedom offers the environment in which those choices can be made without undue restraint.

However, there will be times where your freedom to act will not be easy. Consider the challenges women often face in historically male-dominated roles. If you are in this situation, you might possess the skills and drive (your agency), but societal biases and structural inequalities might restrict your personal freedom to act. Overcoming these barriers requires not just individual agency but also collective action.

EXTERNAL INFLUENCES SHAPE AGENCY

Let's discuss the multifaceted relationship between societal norms, workplace dynamics, and family roles, and their collective impact on a woman's sense of agency and confidence. Insights into how you can navigate and balance these influences will help you as you explore the challenges and opportunities that lie at the intersection of these critical areas of life.

SOCIETAL NORMS

Societal expectations and stereotypes—for example, about "feminine" behavior—can act as barriers to any woman's sense of agency. For example, phrases like "You're too aggressive" or expectations that you should be soft-spoken can undermine you and damage your confidence. You may struggle to navigate these societal expectations while doing your best to stay true to your authentic self. This can be trickier as you rise in organizations and where you may begin to bump into moments that call for you to be bold.

WORKPLACE DYNAMICS

The professional environment, historically dominated by certain leadership models, such as a top-down, authoritative approach, can influence your ability to exercise agency. A supportive culture that encourages diverse styles can bolster your agency. Conversely, a homogenous group might suppress your style.

FAMILY ROLES

Your family, with its dynamics and expectations, plays a significant role in shaping your agency. Support from family, or the lack thereof, can influence professional and personal decisions. For some, exercising agency means challenging or negotiating traditional roles.

By understanding and harnessing the power of agency, you can shape your destiny and ensure that despite external influences, your goals align with your authentic self. I encourage you to:

- Recognize and harness your agency.
- Seek environments that bolster your personal freedom.
- Challenge and negotiate external influences that might restrict your agency.

CONFIDENCE: THE BY-PRODUCT OF AGENCY

Confidence isn't just a trait that some are born with and others lack. It's a quality that can be nurtured and grown, with agency acting as the catalyst. Every choice you make, every risk you take, and every challenge you overcome strengthens your confidence muscle.

Confidence is often likened to a flame. It can start as a mere flicker, but with the right conditions, it can grow into a roaring fire, illuminating your path and providing warmth to those around you. And if you were to trace back to the spark that ignites this flame, more often than not, you would find your agency. This agency—the ability to make choices and act upon them—is the bedrock upon which confidence is built.

Life constantly presents us with crossroads. At each juncture, you face decisions, some trivial and others transformative. And every time you take ownership, making a decision based on your values, beliefs, or goals, you do more than just pick a direction. You reinforce your belief in yourself. You demonstrate to yourself that you are capable and in charge of your destiny. This self-belief then becomes the fuel that powers the flame of confidence. It reaffirms that your voice matters, your choices have power, and you are an active participant in shaping your life's narrative.

For example, Stacy, an experienced health care consulting executive, used her confidence and belief in herself to begin a new career path as part of her bold journey. "When I made the bold move to leave my corporate job and become an entrepreneur, I had to believe that I could provide for my family as the single breadwinner," she says. "Believing in myself was first an inner knowing of my identity, which was based on who I am and what I am called to create—my why—not based on what I did for my job." She credits others in her personal and professional networks for bolstering that self-belief by challenging limiting beliefs and myths she held. "I now know that when I step out in bold action aligned with my belief, goodness will follow," Stacy says.

The relationship between agency and confidence can be visualized as a positive feedback loop. It begins with making a choice, an act of agency. This choice, especially when it leads to a positive outcome, instills confidence. As your confidence grows, you feel  more empowered, more in control, and more willing to make more choices. The cycle continues, with each act of agency bolstering your confidence, and each surge in confidence amplifying your agency.

For instance, consider the decision to speak up in a meeting. The very act of voicing your opinion, of deciding that your thoughts are valuable and worth sharing, is an exercise in agency. When your input is acknowledged or appreciated, your confidence grows. The next time you're in a similar situation, this boosted confidence makes it easier to speak up, further expanding your agency.

REAL-LIFE TALES OF CONFIDENCE AND AGENCY
Confidence and agency play pivotal roles in shaping your personal and professional lives. In your personal life, confidence enables you to assert your needs and desires, build meaningful relationships, and navigate challenges with resilience. In your professional world, having a strong sense of agency empowers you to set ambitious goals, take initiative, and make impactful contributions. These qualities can open doors to greater opportunities and success.

Amy always wanted to travel, but she had a full-time job, a mortgage, and family responsibilities. She liked her tech job but knew it was not aligned with her passion for adventure and travel. She took time to learn more about the travel industry, network, and meet others who had the same passion. She ultimately was able to find a job in the travel industry that leveraged her tech skills and brought her joy and happiness.

Elizabeth was an introvert. The thought of public speaking or even voicing her opinions in a group setting made her anxious. But when she was unexpectedly asked to lead a project presentation, she decided to face her fear. She prepared diligently. It was not flawless, but she did it. That choice to confront her fear, to take control of the situation, gave Elizabeth a confidence boost. Over time, with more experience, her confidence in public speaking grew. Today, she mentors others in effective communication.

Jasmine worked as a financial analyst, a stable and well-paying job, but her true passion lay in cooking. Every evening, she found joy in experimenting with new recipes and cuisines. She realized her dream was to become a chef, but the thought of leaving her secure job was daunting. Jasmine started small. She enrolled in evening culinary classes and began a food blog to document her journey. Gradually, her blog gained followers, and she started catering small events on weekends. Over time, Jasmine's side venture grew, and she felt confident enough to transition into a full-time culinary career, combining her love for cooking with the business skills from her previous job. Today, she has her own catering company.

HOW TO CULTIVATE AGENCY, CONFIDENCE, AND BOLDNESS

The trio of agency, confidence, and boldness set you up for a dynamic journey of self-improvement and achievement. While understanding the theory behind these concepts is vital, the real magic lies in embedding them in your daily life. Here are some practical ways to cultivate and harness these powerful forces.

Make Daily Decisions That Reinforce Agency

- **Begin each day with a deliberate choice.** It could be as simple as picking what to eat for breakfast or as profound as setting an intention for the day. The act of making a conscious decision reinforces your agency, reminding you of your control over your life's narrative.

- **At the end of each day, take a few moments to reflect on the decisions you made.** Assess the outcomes, consider the reasons behind each choice, and celebrate the victories, no matter how small. This practice strengthens agency and fosters learning and growth.

Build Your Confidence

- **Start your day with a positive affirmation.** Affirmations are designed to boost self-confidence. They are short statements typically phrased in the present tense that focus on positive attributes or goals you wish to manifest or reinforce in your life. Statements like "I am in control of my choices" or "I trust my abilities" can set a confident tone for the day. Over time, these affirmations, when repeated with conviction, can reshape your self-perception and boost your confidence.

- **Celebrate small wins.** Confidence grows when you recognize your achievements. Set small, achievable goals, and when you accomplish them, take a moment to relish the victory. It could be completing a challenging task, getting in a workout, or even simply surviving a hectic day.

Reinforce Your Boldness

- **Step out of your comfort zone by embracing new experiences.** Switch up where you take your daily walk, try a new food, or watch a movie in a genre that's new to you. New experiences of any size challenge your beliefs, push your boundaries, and cultivate boldness.

- **Seek constructive feedback from others.** Actively seek feedback on your decisions and actions, especially from trusted peers, mentors, friends, or family. Constructive feedback can offer new perspectives, which may motivate you to make bolder choices.

Consider the story of Tara, a young woman who aspired to lead her team at work. She began by making intentional choices daily, from managing her time effectively (including saying no to tasks) to volunteering for projects outside her job description. These decisions, rooted in her agency, gradually built her confidence. As her confidence grew, she began taking bolder steps, like introducing herself to people in other departments and more actively participating in brainstorming sessions. Over time, her boldness was recognized, and she was promoted to a leadership position. Throughout her journey, Tara took ownership of both successes and setbacks, continually reinforcing her agency and paving the way for growth.

It's a virtuous circle: Your daily decisions, driven by agency, lay the foundation for increasing your confidence. As your confidence surges, it encourages you to take bolder actions. And with every bold step, you take ownership of the outcomes, reinforcing your agency.

ACTIVITY

MY BOLD FACTOR: AGENCY, CONFIDENCE, BOLDNESS, AND OWNERSHIP

This quiz helps you identify your strengths in agency, confidence, boldness, and ownership, providing insight into areas for potential growth and development.

Choose the response that best aligns with your likely action in each scenario. Tally your scores at the end to evaluate your level in each trait.

1. WHEN YOU ARE PRESENTED WITH A NEW PROJECT AT WORK:

A You eagerly take it on, excited about the challenge. **Boldness**

B You analyze whether you have the necessary skills before accepting. **Agency**

C You worry about the new responsibilities. **Neither**

2. WHEN YOU NEED TO MAKE AN IMPORTANT DECISION:

A You trust your gut and decide quickly. **Confidence**

B You take time to gather information and weigh options. **Agency**

C You often ask others to make the decision. **Neither**

3. WHEN YOU RECEIVE NEGATIVE FEEDBACK:

A You see it as an opportunity to improve and grow. **Ownership**

B You may feel discouraged but you know you will learn from it. **Confidence**

C You dismiss it as irrelevant. **Neither**

4. WHEN YOU ARE FACING A TASK OUTSIDE YOUR COMFORT ZONE:

A You feel nervous but give it your best shot. **Confidence**

B You decline or avoid the task. **Neither**

C You embrace the challenge to learn something new. **Boldness**

5. WHEN YOU EXPERIENCE FAILURE:

A You analyze what went wrong and plan for improvement. **Ownership**

B You choose a new path forward and ask for help. **Agency**

C You blame external factors. **Neither**

6. WHEN YOU HAVE THE CHANCE TO LEAD A TEAM:

A You step up, excited for the opportunity. **Boldness**

B You evaluate whether you're the best fit for the role and collaborate as needed. **Agency**

C You feel overwhelmed and prefer someone else to lead. **Neither**

7. WHEN IT'S TIME TO VOICE YOUR OPINION IN A GROUP:

A You speak up confidently, even if what you have to say is unpopular. **Boldness**

B You share your thoughts but ask what others think as well. **Confidence**

C You usually keep your opinions to yourself. **Neither**

8. WHEN YOU ARE DEALING WITH A PERSONAL CHALLENGE:

A You rely on your ability to handle it yourself. **Agency**

B You may feel unsure but try to manage it positively. **Confidence**

C You always seek help from others. **Neither**

9. WHEN YOU HAVE AN OPPORTUNITY TO LEARN A NEW SKILL:

A You are excited and start immediately. **Boldness**

B You consider how this skill can benefit your future. **Agency**

C You doubt your ability to learn it. **Neither**

10. WHEN SOMEONE CHALLENGES YOUR VIEWPOINT:

A You defend your perspective without hesitation. **Confidence**

B You reassess your viewpoint and consider changing it based on new input. **Agency**

C You agree with them to avoid conflict. **Neither**

11. WHEN YOU ARE SETTING PERSONAL GOALS:

A You set ambitious and challenging goals. **Boldness**

B You set realistic and mostly achievable goals. **Agency**

C You rarely set specific goals. **Neither**

12. WHEN YOUR PROJECT DOESN'T GO AS PLANNED:

A You quickly adapt and find new solutions. **Agency**

B You may feel stressed but remain positive you can determine a solution. **Confidence**

C You feel it's not your fault and blame circumstances. **Neither**

13. WHEN YOU HAVE TO WORK ON A COMPLEX PROBLEM:

A You break it down into manageable parts and tackle them systematically. **Agency**

B You feel assured in your ability to solve it. **Confidence**

C You feel overwhelmed and unsure where to start. **Neither**

14. WHEN YOU HAVE THE CHANCE TO NETWORK WITH INFLUENTIAL PEOPLE:

A You feel nervous but see it as a valuable opportunity. **Confidence**

B You actively engage and introduce yourself to new people. **Boldness**

C You stay in your comfort zone, talking to familiar faces. **Neither**

15. WHEN YOU NEED TO BALANCE MULTIPLE RESPONSIBILITIES:

A You prioritize tasks based on importance and deadlines. **Agency**

B You feel capable of managing them effectively. **Confidence**

C You often feel overwhelmed and procrastinate. **Neither**

Scoring:
For each response, give yourself a point under the corresponding trait (Agency, Confidence, or Boldness). Tally your scores for each category.

Outcome:
Agency High scores indicate you're proactive and self-reliant in decision-making.

Confidence High scores reflect trust in your abilities and positive self-perception.

Boldness High scores show you're willing to take risks and embrace challenges.

Ownership High scores indicate that you are able to take responsibility and own your actions.

KEY TAKEAWAYS

Agency is the ability to make choices and exert power in shaping your destiny. It represents the inner strength that enables you to navigate life's challenges.

Confidence is a by-product of agency. Confidence is likened to a flame that grows from the spark of agency. Making decisions based on your personal beliefs, values, or desires reinforces your confidence.

A symbiotic relationship exists between agency, confidence, and decision-making. Agency leads to making choices, which, if positive, boost confidence. Increased confidence then amplifies agency, enhancing decision-making.

Agency, confidence, boldness, and ownership are interconnected. Agency enables decision-making. Decisions build confidence. Confidence leads to boldness. Boldness requires taking ownership of outcomes. Ownership fosters agency. It's a virtuous cycle.

WHAT'S NEXT

Having embraced ownership in this section's chapters, you're now poised to enter the third foundational step in The BOLD Framework: *learn*. This is where the power of making bold choices, fortified by the strength of ownership, meets the expansive potential of knowledge and continuous growth. The next section explores how continuous learning can significantly enhance your bold moves. Think of it this way: If your choices and actions, underpinned by your sense of ownership, are driving you forward, then continuous learning is the fuel that keeps the engine running efficiently and effectively.

Get ready to explore how a perpetual state of curiosity and eagerness to learn can amplify your capacity for boldness. You've built the foundation of agency and ownership, and now you'll enrich it with knowledge, skills, and insights that open up new possibilities.

PART 4

LEARN

It's time to explore the third foundational step of The BOLD Framework: *learn*. You will discover new horizons and grow through setbacks. It is a process of discovery, of setting new directions and bridging gaps. Imagine yourself as an explorer, charting unknown territories with excitement and curiosity.

BOLD MEANS

"Everyone's definition of bold is likely to change over time. In fact, it should. I think bold is listening to our hearts and ignoring the naysayers. It's doing the thing that makes us feel excited, even if it makes us feel a little bit scared. And it's ignoring that little nagging voice of doubt in our heads and going for it!"

—Melissa Cohen, founder of MBC Consulting Solutions

On *The Bold Lounge* Podcast

CHAPTER 10
CONTINUOUS LEARNING CYCLE

"Life is a school where every day is a chance to learn something new."

This chapter kick-starts the third foundational step of The BOLD Framework: *learn*. To thrive in a world of constant change and make desired changes, mere courage or determination is not enough. You need an unyielding commitment to continuous learning. It is this commitment that helps you be nimble and make bold, intentional choices that shape your life's narrative. Learning is where true change, evolution, and growth occurs.

Think of a time when you felt stuck, perhaps even now. It may feel like wandering through a maze, the scenery repetitive and uninspiring. Your comfort zone, once a sanctuary, starts to feel tight and unfulfilling. Staying in this safe space, avoiding risks, fearing mistakes, or settling into complacency—these aren't just symptoms of stagnation. They are also signals that you've hit pause on your learning journey. And when learning halts, so does growth.

Get ready to reignite your learning spirit, break free from the maze, and leap beyond your comfort zone. Learning can transform not just how you think but also how you live.

GET UNSTUCK

You may have had moments where you thought, *Why does this keep happening to me?* or *Why do I keep making the same mistake?* The answer often lies in your approach. If you do not pause to reflect on and learn from your experiences, you risk falling into the same patterns. It is like trying to complete a puzzle without looking at the picture on the box. Without perspective and learning, you're merely shuffling pieces around, hoping they will fit.

The key to breaking free from this cycle, to truly embracing risk, growth, and boldness, is to immerse yourself in continuous learning. By continuously learning, reflecting, and applying newfound knowledge, you fill your bold journey with purpose, passion, and potential.

The idea of continuous learning might sound daunting if you picture formal education, complete with scheduled class times and final exams. But the beauty of continuous learning is that it's woven into the fabric of daily life. You learn from every conversation, experience, and, yes, mistake.

"I think of bold as being authentic, confident, and open to varied ideas, perspectives, and opportunities. It is being curious—asking deep questions of yourself and others to learn more and do better. And it is taking calculated risks, failing forward, and continuing to grow."
—Melissa Lewis-Stoner, VP of product management at Relias

For instance, Sara, a mother of two with a passion for sustainable fashion, loved reading fashion blogs, magazines, and books. She followed leaders in the industry on social media. She wanted to make her own impact on the world of fashion, so she created a blog. Seeing its success, she thought about creating a full website. Sara sought feedback and attended workshops. She learned what didn't work as well as what did. As she learned and adapted, her impact grew. Today, her very popular blog and website demonstrate the power of continuous learning.

Sara's journey underscores a vital lesson: growth isn't just about moving forward. It is also about expanding, evolving, and embracing new dimensions of yourself. Whether it's picking up a new skill, understanding a different perspective, or simply being curious, every act of learning adds a layer to your personal and professional growth.

ADAPTING SUPPORTS FORWARD MOTION

Imagine you are on a hike and suddenly the path you are on is blocked. Do you turn back or do you find another way? Life is a lot like that hike. Things change, obstacles pop up, and the path isn't always clear. But if you're someone who can quickly adapt and learn new things, you will find it easier to move forward.

We all have those "oops!" moments. Maybe you forgot an appointment, or perhaps a project didn't go as planned. It's easy to get upset. But what if, instead, you forgave yourself, gave yourself permission to move on, and, most importantly, looked at these moments as chances to adapt and learn? A chance to look up and notice what is working and not working? A chance to learn and come back even stronger and with more energy? This is a choice.

In this rapidly evolving world, adaptability and continuous learning are more than just concepts to ponder. They can determine your success in your personal and professional lives. The more you engage in them, the more they will become integral parts of your daily life. Here are strategies that can help you practice being adaptable.

STAY CURIOUS

As an adult, it's easy to get caught up in routines and forget that sense of wonder, and the endless list of questions that went along with it that you had as a child. But staying curious, asking questions, and seeking answers are the very essence of learning. Whether it's about a new technology, an unfamiliar place, or local politics, work to keep that inquisitive spirit alive. The more questions you ask, the broader your horizons become.

TRY NEW THINGS

Your comfort zone is, well, comfortable, but nothing grows there, including you. Trying new things—whether it's picking up a new hobby, like jewelry making or snowboarding, experimenting with a different approach at work, or tasting a cuisine you've never tried before—can be fun and enlightening. Doing new things strengthens resilience, exposes you to different perspectives, and often leads to unexpected discoveries.

TALK TO DIFFERENT PEOPLE

Every individual is a repository of experiences, stories, and knowledge. Engaging in conversations with people from diverse backgrounds or demographics can be immensely enriching. It helps break biases, introduces you to fresh perspectives, and often leads to collaborative learning. So, the next time you are at a social gathering, a workshop, or even in a virtual meet, try to engage with someone you wouldn't typically speak to.

"Knowledge grows when courage meets curiosity."

ACTIVITY
EXPLORE SOMETHING NEW

This activity will reignite your curiosity, encourage stepping out of your comfort zone, and foster meaningful interactions. You will broaden your knowledge and experiences and enhance your adaptability and openness to continuous learning. Over the next few weeks, complete this series of tasks and reflections aimed at stimulating your mind and soul.

WEEK 1: EMBRACE CURIOSITY

▸ Choose a topic you know little about but find intriguing and want to learn more.

▸ Spend the week researching this topic. This could involve reading articles, watching documentaries, or listening to podcasts. Aim to learn something new about it each day. Take notes about what you learn. Also, observe how it feels to learn. Are you happier? Do you feel more engaged? Is it fun?

▸ At the end of the week, write down how gaining new knowledge has affected you. Has it changed your perspective or inspired you to further pursue the topic or something related to it?

WEEK 2: STEP OUT OF YOUR COMFORT ZONE

▸ Identify an activity or skill outside of your comfort zone. It could be going bowling or doing a yoga video, reading a different genre of books, or speaking to a new colleague.

▸ Try to engage in this activity two or three times during the week. (It can also be a one-off, like joining a friend's trivia team for an evening.) Focus on the process rather than the outcome.

▸ At the end of the week, write about how stepping out of your comfort zone made you feel. Did you feel challenged? Nervous? Excited?

WEEK 3: ENGAGE WITH DIVERSE INDIVIDUALS

▶ Strike up a conversation with at least three people who are different from you in some significant way (culture, role, experience, profession, age, etc.).

▶ In each conversation, aim to learn something new or gain a different perspective. Ask open-ended questions and listen actively.

▶ At the end of the week, write about the insights you gained from these interactions. Did any of these conversations challenge your preconceptions or open your mind to new ideas?

ONGOING: INTEGRATE AND ADAPT

▶ Integrate the insights and skills you have gained into your daily life. This could mean applying knowledge from your research, continuing with the new activity, or maintaining connections with the people you've met.

▶ Continue to seek out new experiences, topics, and connections.

▶ Regularly reflect on your growth. How are these experiences shaping you? How are you adapting to new challenges and information?

"Think of learning as an adventure, always discovering something exciting."

GROWTH MINDSET AS A CATALYST

While continuous learning is the action, the growth mindset, which we discussed in chapter 2, is the belief system that invigorates this action. The term "growth mindset" refers to the belief that abilities and intelligence can be developed through dedication and hard work. With a growth mindset, you view challenges as opportunities to learn. You understand that effort plays a crucial role in achieving mastery and that failures are lessons, not setbacks. A growth mindset contrasts with a fixed mindset, where you believe that your abilities are static and cannot be changed. Such a belief system can be limiting, leading to avoidance of challenges and a fear of failure.

For continuous learners, having a growth mindset is indispensable. It's the growth mindset that pushes you to venture out of your comfort zone, seek new experiences, and venture into the unknown. It's this mindset that tells you that not knowing something isn't a weakness but an opportunity to learn. It supports the belief that learning, effort, and perseverance will help you achieve your goals.

Being a continuous learner and having a growth mindset are closely connected. The growth mindset serves as the foundation, the belief system that prods you to seek continuous learning. Continuous learning reinforces the growth mindset. They feed off each other, creating a virtuous cycle. Every time you face a challenge, overcome it, and learn from it, it strengthens your belief in the power of learning. Continuously learning, adapting, and growing can inspire those around you to do the same.

THE POWER OF ADAPTABILITY AND CONTINUOUS LEARNING

Adaptability and continuous learning are lifelines that enable growth, transformation, and fulfillment.

For example, when journalism expanded to include podcasts and videos, Maria, a print journalist, chose to embrace the change and adapt. She enrolled in digital media courses and used online resources to learn the ropes of multimedia content creation.

Emily, a busy senior executive, had a health scare that made her reevaluate her lifestyle choices. Continuous learning about nutrition and well-being became her ally. Instead of drastic resolutions, she chose to successfully adapt to a healthier lifestyle by making small, sustainable changes, like taking daily walks and choosing healthier food options.

When you embrace change and cherish the lessons it brings, you are crafting your own narrative, which illuminates the endless possibilities that life offers you. The hardest part sometimes is to remember learning is a choice and to not miss chances to learn because you get bogged down in routine.

Each day offers lessons waiting to be discovered and integrated into your bold journey. From having a casual conversation with a friend to navigating politics at work, daily lessons are everywhere. But you have to be open to notice them and recognize the invaluable insight and wisdom they offer. It is an intentional choice.

TRANSFORM CHALLENGES INTO OPPORTUNITIES

While the initial sting of a misstep might cause you to be disappointed or upset, a deeper dive often reveals an invaluable lesson.

Remember Maria, the journalist who added multimedia skills to her résumé? There were new tools to learn, evolving algorithms to understand, and increasingly savvy digital audience to connect with. Her challenges in adapting to the expanded digital publishing world became opportunities for growth.

Linda, after a failed business venture, gained insights that allowed her to establish a much more successful enterprise later on. Stephanie faced numerous rejections before her innovative idea gained traction and became a game-changer in her industry. Their stories underline a universal truth that challenges, when approached with a growth mindset, can lead to what would otherwise be missed opportunities.

The power of learning cannot be overstated. It is the key that unlocks doors and helps you venture beyond your comfort zone. Life throws curveballs when least expected. A growth mindset and continuous learning allow you to adapt to changing scenarios and become more resilient.

Learning is not just about acquiring new knowledge. It is equally about the ability to unlearn habits that do not help and relearn or replace them with more effective ones. This cycle of learning and relearning is crucial for keeping up in our ever-evolving world.

KEY TAKEAWAYS

Continuous learning is essential for navigating life's ever-changing terrain. Learning opportunities are woven into the fabric of daily life. Learning allows you to adapt and make bold, intentional choices.

Feeling stuck is often a sign of ceased learning. Continuous learning is the key to breaking free from repetitive patterns, allowing for personal growth and development.

You can choose to view every mistake and challenge as a learning opportunity. This mindset transforms potential setbacks into valuable learning experiences.

Practice being adaptable and look for new ways to learn. Strategies include being curious, trying new things, and talking to different people.

If you have a growth mindset, you believe that you can develop your abilities through effort and learning. This mindset is essential for continuous learners.

WHAT'S NEXT

Think back to a time when things didn't go as planned. Perhaps a goal that seemed within reach suddenly became unattainable, or a well-laid plan took an unexpected turn. The next chapter will explore how these unexpected, often challenging turns can lead to better outcomes than originally imagined, increase your adaptability, and strengthen your resilience. Redirection is about more than just making the best of a situation. It's about actively reshaping your journey toward success.

BOLD MEANS

"Living, thinking, speaking in ways that are courageous and unapologetic. For me, that can look like being true to who I am no matter what space I'm in . . . unapologetically chasing my passion and the things that bring me joy versus chasing the things that culture, society, the world tells me I should chase."

—Ariel Belgrave Harris, award-winning health and fitness coach

On *The Bold Lounge* Podcast

CHAPTER 11
THE POWER OF REDIRECTION

"Redirection is the art of reshaping our narrative, transforming challenges into chapters of learning and growth."

The previous chapter kicked off the third foundational step: *learn*. This chapter focuses on an important learning tool: redirection. Redirection is not just about course correction. It is about seizing control of the narrative when life takes an unexpected turn. Redirection can recast setbacks into springboards, disappointments into discoveries, and challenges into opportunities. You'll also explore how adaptability and resilience support the transformative power of redirection.

ACKNOWLEDGE DISAPPOINTMENT

When things do not go according to plan, it is natural to feel a sense of disappointment. You may have worked tirelessly toward a goal, only to see it slip away. Acknowledge your feelings of disappointment. It's okay to be upset, frustrated, or disheartened. Give yourself the space to feel these emotions fully. Bottling them up or pretending they don't exist can be counterproductive. By acknowledging the feelings, you can begin to understand clearly what you own or do not own, as well as be open to redirection.

Once you have acknowledged your disappointment, it's time to shift your perspective. Instead of seeing a setback as a dead end, view it as a detour, a different path that can lead you to unexpected and exciting places. It could lead you to your original goal, but it might lead you to a new, bolder goal you did not originally set for yourself.

Consider the story of Susan, who had her sights set on becoming the CEO of a major tech company. She had worked tirelessly for years, moving up the corporate ladder, only to be passed over after being considered and going through multiple rounds of interviews. At first, she felt crushed by this setback. Then Susan decided to shift her perspective. She realized that not getting the CEO position gave her the opportunity to explore other aspects of her professional and personal life.

Susan took on new projects, connected with different people in her industry, and started a mentoring program for young women in tech. Over time, she found immense fulfillment in these activities. She realized that her initial disappointment had opened doors she had not even considered before. She became a highly respected leader in her field, albeit not in the way she had originally planned.

Susan's story illustrates the power of redirection, of shifting your perspective. By reframing setbacks as opportunities, you can uncover new passions, talents, and paths you might never have explored otherwise.

ACTIVITY
MAKE A REDIRECTION PLAN

This activity will help you practice redirecting a setback into a new route for success. The process demonstrates a proactive approach to overcoming challenges and finding alternative paths.

1. IDENTIFY A SETBACK

▷ Think of a recent setback you faced that represents an ongoing challenge you want to change; for example, maybe you missed a deadline or received negative feedback.

▷ Write a detailed description of the setback, including what happened, how it affected you, and why it felt like a setback.

2. REFLECT ON THE EXPERIENCE

▷ Reread what you wrote and spend some time reflecting on it as an example of an ongoing challenge.

▷ Write your answers to the following questions:
  • What were my initial reactions to this setback?
  • What did I learn from this experience?
  • Were there positive aspects or opportunities that emerged?
  • How did this setback affect my goals?

3. EXPLORE ALTERNATIVE PATHS

▷ Spend fifteen minutes brainstorming alternative ways to approach your ongoing challenge. Write down as many ways as possible in the time allotted. Don't judge or edit your ideas. Include unconventional approaches and ones that may not seem attainable on first take. Pick three strategies to consider in more detail.

4. DEVELOP A REDIRECTION PLAN

▸ Choose one of the three approaches to focus on first. (You can always revisit the other ones.)

▸ Write down a detailed plan for this new direction. Include specific steps, resources needed, and a timeline. Don't try to change overnight or overcomplicate your plan. Set attainable short-term goals that will move you forward and help you successfully change incrementally over time.

5. IMPLEMENT AND ADAPT

▸ Take the first step outlined in your plan. When you're done with that one step, check it off and move on to the next. Consider scheduling time in your calendar for each step. Be prepared to adapt as you progress, staying flexible as you gather new information or changes in circumstances occur.

6. REFLECT AND ADJUST

▸ At the end of each week, review and record your progress. Ask yourself:
  - What successes did I achieve this week?
  - What challenges did I encounter, and how did I address them?
  - Do I need to make any adjustments to my plan based on what I've learned?

7. CELEBRATE PROGRESS

▸ Acknowledge and celebrate your progress. Give yourself credit for all victories, large and small. Celebrating progress can boost your morale and motivation to continue.

"Through redirection, we learn that the unexpected turns of life are not just detours, but destinations of new understanding."

THE POWER OF ADAPTABILITY AND RESILIENCE

Adaptability and resilience are superpowers that support the process of redirection. When faced with setbacks, these qualities can make all the difference in your ability to thrive.

We talked about adaptability, being flexible and open to change, in the last chapter. It means being willing to pivot when your initial plan does not work out. It might involve learning new skills, exploring different paths, or adjusting your goal.

Resilience is your ability to bounce back from adversity. Resilience enables you to keep moving forward, even when you face setbacks. It's about learning from your experiences, growing stronger, and using that strength to push yourself toward your goal.

Rita, for example, had worked for a company for almost ten years and had high hopes of becoming a senior leader there. Then a surprising layoff completely rocked her world, her confidence, and her plan. Rita was devastated, but she refused to let this failure define her. Backed by her adaptability and resilience, she chose to view this as a transition time during which she could gain more knowledge and reset her work-life alignment. Rita then took on a leadership role at a different organization, where she is now even more successful.

CAREER REINVENTION

Aligning your passion with your work can be part of the process of redirection. Sometimes a job loss provides the nudge you need to realign your career with your authentic self.

Losing your job unexpectedly can be one of life's most challenging curveballs, especially in the moment. It can feel devastating and disorienting. Suddenly, the routine you have grown accustomed to vanishes, leaving you with a sense of loss and confusion. You may feel a range of other emotions, such as fear, doubt, and anger. However, such transitions can lead to remarkable career reinvention. It's a time when you can discover talents and passions you may have overlooked or that had gone dormant while you were caught up in the demands of your previous role.

For example, Ingrid had spent over a decade as a senior leader in a high-pressure real estate agency. She was passionate about her work but had little time for anything else. Then Ingrid was let go. At first, she felt lost without her job and the identity it had given her. However, after her initial shock, Ingrid decided to make a fresh start. She realized that she missed doing hands-on creative work and decided to return to writing, where she had started her career. She repositioned herself as a freelance copywriter. To her surprise, she found both joy and success in her newfound pursuit. She also thrived in the much less stressful environment of working from home.

Likewise, Marisol, a software engineer, was laid off after a decade in the tech industry. Initially, she was anxious about her future. But she took the time to evaluate and realized that she had always been passionate about education. Marisol decided to pursue a career in education technology, combining her technical skills with her love for teaching. A company that was aligned with her purpose and values hired her to work on educational apps.

Losing your job can be an invitation to reflect on your career, but you don't need to wait for a crisis to prompt this introspection. On a regular basis, ask yourself, *What do I really love to do? What gives me a sense of purpose and fulfillment?* When you answer these questions honestly, you take the steps toward aligning your career with your true self. Following are more ways to spark career reinvention.

"Redirection isn't a setback. It's a classroom where resilience and adaptability become our greatest teachers."

MAKE THE MOST OF YOUR CURRENT ROLE

At times, you may feel stuck or unfulfilled in your current job, especially if it doesn't exactly align with your long-term goals or passions. However, rather than viewing your job as a dead end, redirect your perspective and consider it as a platform for growth and learning.

Lauren, for example, worked as a customer service representative at a retail company. At first glance, her job seemed far removed from her dream of becoming a marketing manager. However, Lauren decided to reset her perspective. She recognized that her role provided valuable opportunities to improve her communication and problem-solving skills. Lauren also took the initiative to introduce herself to the marketing team, which led to her collaborating with them on small projects during her free time. Her insights on customer preferences proved valuable in shaping marketing strategies. Eventually, her proactive approach and the skills she acquired in her customer service role earned her a promotion to a marketing associate position. By making the most of her current role and finding ways to connect it with her long-term goals, Lauren turned what could have been a stagnant position into the next level of her career.

It's easy to get bogged down in daily routines, such as completing work tasks that do not reflect your potential. If this is the case, think about how you can apply redirection by redesigning or innovating aspects of your work to showcase your talents.

Take the example of Alex, a project manager who oversaw multiple teams. While she excelled in project management, she also had a knack for creative problem-solving and design. She noticed that client reports were often stale and uninspiring. Alex sought permission to redesign the report templates, adding visually engaging elements and infographics to make the data more accessible. Her revamped reports impressed clients. They also made it easier for internal teams to understand what other teams were doing. By finding ways to incorporate her complementary talents into her existing role, Alex improved her job satisfaction and enhanced her value to the company.

TAKE SMALL, PRACTICAL STEPS

Redirecting is not limited to your professional life. It extends to your daily routines and personal experiences as well. By adopting a positive outlook and seeking opportunities for growth in everyday situations, you can create a more fulfilling life.

Consider daily exercise. Instead of viewing it as a chore, reset it as a chance to boost your energy, clear your mind, and improve your overall health. You can also rethink how, when, and where you exercise. If you're not working out because you don't have time to go to the gym, for example, sneak in exercise "breaks" throughout the day. Do squats while you wait for the microwave, take the stairs, and park farther away from the door. Shifts in perspective can make exercise a more enjoyable and sustainable habit.

Likewise, you can apply redirection to how you view household chores. Instead of resenting them, look at them as opportunities to practice mindfulness or listen to your favorite podcasts. By turning routine tasks into enjoyable moments, you can make the most of your time and create a more positive mindset.

LISTEN TO YOUR INNER VOICE

While making the most of your current situation is valuable, there may come a time when you listen to your inner voice, which we talked about in chapter 1, and realize you need or desire a more significant personal or professional change. This awareness is a quiet, bold step toward exploring new possibilities. Ask yourself questions like, *What truly brings me happiness and fulfillment? Am I aligned with my authentic self? What changes can I make to live a more purposeful life?*

Emma, for example, had spent years as a corporate lawyer, pursuing a stable and high-paying career. However, as she approached her forties, she began to feel a growing disconnect between her job and her mission to help others. She realized that what truly brought her joy was working with animals and promoting animal welfare. Emma researched opportunities in the animal welfare sector and began volunteering at local shelters. Her passion and dedication caught the attention of organizations in the field, and she eventually transitioned to a career focused on animal welfare advocacy. By recognizing her need for change and taking steps toward exploring new possibilities, Emma discovered a more fulfilling career that aligned with her purpose and passion.

PURSUE WHAT BRINGS YOU JOY

In the quest for personal and professional growth on your bold journey, think about what truly brings you happiness and fulfillment. Consider activities or interests that genuinely excite you. What do you lose track of time doing? What brings you a sense of purpose and joy? These are clues to your passions.

Once you have identified your passions and areas where you would like to explore new possibilities, taking the initial steps can be both exhilarating and daunting. Change often involves stepping out of your comfort zone and embracing uncertainty.

A helpful approach is to break down your larger goals into smaller, manageable steps. This makes a transition more achievable and allows you to celebrate your progress along the way. For instance, if you are considering a career change, start by researching the industry you are interested in, networking with professionals in that field, or taking courses to acquire necessary skills. These smaller steps can build the foundation for more significant, bolder changes.

STRENGTHEN RELATIONSHIPS THROUGH REDIRECTION

You can also apply redirection to improve your relationships by acknowledging and addressing any challenging issues. The positive impact of such redirection often leads to stronger emotional bonds and increased trust.

For example, Jessica had a strained relationship with her sister, Tori. They had grown apart over the years due to differences in lifestyle and priorities. Jessica initiated an open and honest conversation with Tori, expressing her desire to strengthen their bond. They discussed their differences, found common ground, and committed to making an effort to spend more time together. Their relationship improved, and they discovered a renewed sense of closeness. It seems simple, but making this move was bold. Calling out when your relationships are not working is hard to do, regardless of who it is.

Another example is Mark and Sophia. After being married for over a decade, they realized that their communication had become strained, leading to frequent arguments and misunderstandings. Instead of resigning themselves to the turmoil, they decided to address the issue head-on. Mark and Sophia sought the assistance of a relationship counselor, who guided them through effective communication techniques and conflict-resolution strategies. They learned to listen to each other more empathetically and express their needs and feelings more openly. Over time, their relationship transformed into a healthier and more fulfilling partnership. They learned to appreciate each other's perspectives and found renewed joy in their connection.

Redirection in relationships can both benefit the relationship itself and have a profound impact on your mental and emotional well-being. Unresolved conflicts and strained relationships can cause stress, anxiety, and emotional turmoil. By acknowledging and addressing relationship issues, you create a space for healing and personal growth. The process of working through challenges, communicating openly, and finding common ground can bring a sense of relief and improved overall well-being.

KEY TAKEAWAYS

Redirection is more than just course correction. It's about seizing control and turning setbacks into opportunities.

Acknowledge and accept your feelings of disappointment when things don't go as planned. This is the first step toward constructive redirection.

Shift your perspective to see setbacks as opportunities. They are not dead ends. They are detours leading to new paths and possibilities.

Adaptability and resilience are key traits for redirecting setbacks into setups for success. Adaptability involves being open to change and flexible in your outlook and approach. Resilience is the ability to bounce back from difficulties.

Applying redirection to relationship challenges can positively impact your mental and emotional well-being. Strengthening your connections with others leads to an improved quality of life.

WHAT'S NEXT

The next chapter focuses in more detail on how you can effectively use redirection to transform setbacks into opportunities for greater success. You will practice reframing situations, leveraging your current position, and utilizing your strengths. In the dynamic and often unpredictable journey of life, redirection can be key to uncovering hidden potential in unexpected situations. Setbacks and challenges are vital parts of your bold journey that offer unique opportunities to unlock your true potential.

BOLD MEANS

"I think of bold as being this perfect, beautiful marriage between courage and authenticity. It is being able—in the face of feeling fear, in the face of feeling discomfort—to step into action, acting in alignment with a belief that you feel is true and resonant in your heart of hearts. It takes a bold move to remain in resonance with you, being in congruence with your authentic self."

—Cassandra Worthy, world's leading expert on Change Enthusiasm, Founder and CEO of Change Enthusiasm Global, and author of *Change Enthusiasm: How to Harness the Power of Emotion for Leadership and Success*

On *The Bold Lounge* Podcast

CHAPTER 12
UNLOCK YOUR POTENTIAL

"Your potential thrives on bold steps."

As part of the third foundational step of The BOLD Framework—*learn*—you embraced continuous learning in chapter 10 and discovered the transformative power of redirection in chapter 11. This chapter focuses on another key part of learning: unlocking your potential. It's about recognizing your untapped abilities and actively harnessing them to move forward on your bold journey.

Think of it this way: You hold a key, not to a door that leads somewhere unknown, but to expanding the horizons you already see before you. This key isn't hidden or out of reach. It is already in your hands, ready to be used.

The key is knowledge. However, this is not just about accumulating facts and figures but strategically applying what you learn to carve out your own unique path. This chapter will guide you in transforming your knowledge, personal strengths, and everyday learning into tangible, real-world achievements.

WHAT IS POTENTIAL?

At its core, *potential* represents the capacity to become or develop into something in the future. It is the latent qualities or abilities that may be developed and lead to future success or usefulness. In essence, your potential is an uncharted territory of your capabilities and future achievements.

Potential is like a seed. Just as a seed holds the promise of a plant, you possesses the raw ingredients for growth and accomplishment. However, potential is not just about what you can do. It is also about what you can do under the right conditions. It is a blend of factors that include your innate abilities, learned skills, and willingness to grow and adapt.

To define potential in practical terms, you measure the gap between where you are now and where you could be. You envision a future version of yourself that is more skilled, experienced, and accomplished. This vision is not a fantasy. It is a realistic assessment of what you can achieve with effort, learning, and perseverance.

Recognizing when you are not meeting your potential can be challenging, partly because it often requires honest self-reflection. Signs that you might not be reaching your potential include a persistent feeling of underachievement, a lack of fulfillment in your work or personal life, and the sense that your skills and talents are not being fully utilized or challenged. You might feel bored or stuck in a rut. Underutilizing your potential might also manifest as a constant curiosity or feeling that there's something more you could be doing, but you are not quite sure what it is or how to get there.

Understanding unmet potential also involves recognizing barriers that hold you back. These could be external, such as limited opportunities or resources, or internal, like fear of failure or a lack of self-confidence. Identifying and overcoming these barriers involves setting realistic goals, seeking out opportunities for growth, and cultivating a mindset that embraces challenges as opportunities to learn and improve.

Ultimately, potential is a dynamic state, not a fixed point. It expands as you grow and learn. The journey to realizing your potential is ongoing and requires a commitment to self-improvement and a willingness to step out of your comfort zone. By embracing this as part of you bold journey, you open the door to not just achieving more, but also to a deeper understanding of your capabilities and a greater sense of fulfillment in your pursuits.

"Potential grows with boldness."

BRIDGING THE GAP: CURRENT STATE VS. DESIRED STATE
Unlocking your potential involves moving from your current state to a desired state. Your desired state reflects the future you, who is successfully making changes and achieving desired goals. Continuous learning plays a crucial role in bridging the gap between these two states.

To bridge the gap, you must first recognize the gaps that exist. Here are some types of gaps that can impede progress or serve as opportunities for growth.

- The *skills gap* highlights the disparity between your current skill set and the skills necessary to reach your desired state.
- The *experience gap* is the discrepancy between your current experiences and those required to attain your goals.
- The *mindset gap* is a mental challenge that often stems from a fixed mindset, which hinders your willingness to learn, adapt, and embrace change.
- The *resource gap* is a practical hurdle. It revolves around the scarcity and accessibility of essential resources or support required to transition from your current state to your desired one.
- The *values alignment gap* involves ensuring that your core beliefs and values align with your goals.

MAP YOUR POTENTIAL

Making a vision board that captures ways to unlock your potential can help you bridge the gap between your current and desired states in an engaging and inspiring way. Your vision board will serve as a daily visual reminder of your goals and the steps you need to take to achieve them. It's a creative way to keep your aspirations and the necessary actions to reach them at the forefront of your mind, encouraging consistent reflection and motivation.

1. PREPARE YOUR MATERIALS

▶ Get a large sheet of paper or a poster board. Have some colored markers or pens on hand. Sticky notes in various colors are also helpful.

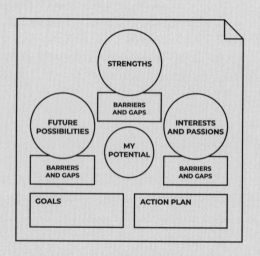

2. DRAW THE CENTRAL THEME

▶ In the center of your paper, draw a large circle. Write "My Potential" inside this circle.

3. CREATE SECTIONS FOR STRENGTHS, INTERESTS, AND POSSIBILITIES

▶ Draw three separate large circles, positioned to the left of, above, and to the right of the central circle. Label these circles as "Strengths," "Interests and Passions," and "Future Possibilities."

4. FILL IN DETAILS

▶ In the "Strengths" circle, list skills, talents, and positive character traits.

- In the "Interests and Passions" circle, list activities or subjects that excite and energize you.
- In the "Future Possibilities" circle, list areas you wish to explore or skills you want to develop.

5. IDENTIFY GAPS AND BARRIERS

- Below each circle, draw a box and label it "Barriers and Gaps."
- Inside this box, list obstacles you feel are holding you back.

6. GOAL-SETTING AREA

- Wherever you have room, draw a column or a box and label it "Goals."
- Write down a few goals that will tap your strengths and reflect your interests and passions. The entries in the Future Possibilities circle can serve as inspirations. Choose one of the goals where you can quickly make progress and highlight it (e.g., with stars).

7. ACTION PLAN SECTION

- Near the Goals area, add another column or box and label it "Action Plan."
- List small, actionable steps to achieve your first goal, along with timelines.

8. DECORATE AND PERSONALIZE

- Add decorative elements, like icons, arrows, or doodles, to make your vision board more engaging. You can also incorporate other visual elements, such as photos.

9. REGULAR UPDATES

- Update your map (e.g., with sticky notes) as you check off or add steps or as your goals evolve.

VISUAL TIPS

▸ **Use color coding.** Assign a different color for each section to visually distinguish them.

▸ **Be creative.** The vision board should reflect your personality, so feel free to get creative.

▸ **Keep it visible.** Place your map somewhere you can see it regularly to help you stay motivated.

IDENTIFY AND EMBRACE YOUR STRENGTHS

Potential is a dynamic force, not a limited quantity. To better understand your potential, identify your unique strengths. Your strengths encompass, for example, your professional and interpersonal skills, personal qualities, talents, expertise, and knowledge. Reflect on what you excel at, what sets you apart. While professional skills are crucial, your strengths extend far beyond the workplace. For example, empathy helps you connect with others on a deep level, building trust and cooperation. Resilience allows you to bounce back from setbacks and lead by example during tough times. Creativity promotes innovative problem-solving and helps you envision new possibilities.

To help identify your strengths, here are some aspects of yourself to consider:

- **Professional skills:** These are the skills you've gained through education, training, and work experience. They encompass, for example, your technical skills, problem-solving abilities, and knowledge in your field.

- **Personal qualities:** These are the qualities that reflect your character. They include traits like empathy, resilience, creativity, adaptability, and authenticity. These traits are the core of your personality.

- **Interpersonal skills:** How well do you connect with and motivate others? Think about your communication skills, emotional intelligence, active listening, and ability to work (and play) well with others.
- **Leadership attributes:** These qualities may include vision, integrity, decisiveness, and the ability to motivate.

Recognizing your strengths goes beyond listing your skills. It is a deep form of reflecting on and acknowledging the talents and personal qualities that have propelled you forward. Think about your achievements, both big and small. What attributes helped you reach these accomplishments? What traits have assisted you in overcoming challenges?

Consider the compliments and feedback you've received from those around you. They often hold clues about your strengths. Ask trusted friends, mentors, and colleagues for their perspectives. They might see strengths in you that you haven't fully realized or appreciated.

"Unlocking your potential begins with the simple belief that you are capable of more."

Your strengths aren't something to hide or downplay. They are something to celebrate and use to your advantage. They empower you and inspire those around you. Embrace them wholeheartedly.

Your strengths will evolve and grow as you continue to learn and develop. Keep nurturing your strengths by seeking learning opportunities that will enhance them. Surround yourself with a supportive network that recognizes and encourages you to optimize your abilities. Embracing your strengths is part of your authenticity and your commitment to live with purpose and integrity.

THE STRENGTHS-BASED APPROACH

Once you have identified and embraced your strengths, experiment with applying a strengths-based approach to your bold journey. This approach involves leveraging your strengths to achieve your goals and positively influence others. When you live with authenticity and a strengths-focused mindset, you become a catalyst for positive change, transforming your own potential into reality and empowering those around you to do the same.

Here are ways you can put your strengths to work:

- **Maximize your impact.** Identify opportunities to apply your strengths. For example, if you excel in communication, use this strength to foster open and effective communication within groups and one-on-one in relationships.

- **Live authentically.** Authenticity is rooted in being true to yourself and embracing your strengths. When you live authentically, you inspire trust and authenticity in others.

- **Collaborate effectively.** Recognize that your strengths complement the strengths of others. Collaboration involves harnessing collective strengths to achieve shared objectives.

- **Provide mentorship and coaching.** Consider sharing your knowledge and strengths by mentoring others. Mentorship not only benefits mentees but also allows you to reinforce your own expertise.

For example, Nina, a seasoned project manager, recognized her strengths in organization, attention to detail, and problem-solving. She embraced these strengths through meticulous, detailed planning. Her problem-solving skills were instrumental in navigating challenges, and she used her organizational abilities to streamline workflows. Nina's team not only met their goals but also exceeded them, thanks to her strengths-based leadership.

STRATEGIES FOR TAKING BOLD ACTION

Tapping into your potential requires action. Action is the catalyst that transforms potential into reality. It requires taking intentional steps toward your goals and aspirations and effecting change in your life.

In setting goals, review your personal definitions of "bold" and "success" from chapter 2. Set audacious goals that challenge and inspire you and reflect your deepest aspirations and values. Dare to dream big and envision the impact you can make. Whether it's breaking glass ceilings, championing social causes, or leading with integrity, your goals should ignite your passion and fuel your determination. The growth, learning, and transformation that occur along the way are equally valuable. Embrace the process, celebrate your progress, and keep your eyes fixed on your goals and dreams.

Start by breaking down each goal into small, manageable, actionable steps, like you did with your vision board. Then, take the first step, no matter how small it may seem. In fact, make it small and celebrate your first win! Each action you take brings you closer to realizing your potential. (In part 5, you will take the fourth foundational step in The BOLD Framework—*design*—and create a life plan that includes more detailed goals and action plans.)

Here are ways to tap into your potential, call on your strengths, and take action toward the life you want to live.

- **Decision-making:** Develop the ability to make decisions confidently and swiftly. Consider the available information, consult when necessary, and trust your judgment.
- **Risk-taking:** Don't shy away from calculated risks. Assess potential outcomes, weigh the pros and cons, and be willing to venture into the unknown when it aligns with your vision.
- **Leadership:** Set the tone by demonstrating the behaviors and work ethic you expect from others.

- **Adaptability:** Be open to change and innovation. Adapt your strategies as needed to respond to evolving circumstances and opportunities.
- **Collaboration:** Encourage collaboration and teamwork. Building a supportive environment empowers others to take bold action as well.

Your story is an evolving narrative shaped by your commitment to learning and your determination to bridge those gaps. You have seen how embracing challenges and actively seeking opportunities to learn can lead to growth and build resilience. With this understanding, you are equipped to move forward on your bold journey, capitalizing on your potential and transcending the confines of your experiences and limitations. Be open to the process, embracing the joy of learning and unlocking your potential, and have the courage to follow a path that resonates with your passions and aspirations.

KEY TAKEAWAYS

Strategically apply knowledge. Application of knowledge enables you to unlock your potential and new opportunities, paving the way to success.

Potential is a dynamic force rather than a fixed quantity. Recognize and cultivate your innate abilities.

Employ a strengths-based approach. Identify and use your unique strengths as tools for positive change.

Adapt and take bold action. Adapt in the face of change, embrace risk-taking, and take bold, decisive actions toward your goals.

WHAT'S NEXT

The next section focuses on the fourth foundational step in The BOLD Framework: *design*. This step involves putting into practice everything you have learned about yourself and your potential. You'll apply these insights to create a life that truly reflects your beliefs, values, and goals.

Designing your life is a process of aligning your day-to-day actions with your long-term vision. This is about making deliberate choices and setting realistic, yet ambitious goals that inspire you and challenge you to grow. These goals will be your guideposts as you navigate your bold journey. Move forward with focus and determination. It's time to turn your goals into reality.

PART 5

DESIGN

It's time to focus on the final foundational step of The BOLD Framework: *design*. This is the culmination of your journey. Here, you will weave together your life plan, building momentum and detailing your action steps. You will balance what you have learned and what you aspire to achieve, crafting a life that aligns with your true self, not just in theory but in practice.

BOLD MEANS

"Being bold is taking risks.
I have never been afraid
to zig when others have
zagged. I call those heartbeat
moments. I follow my
heart, not my head. Doing
something that has not been
done before can be very
scary, but if you don't try, you
will never know. The worst
thing that can happen is you
might be wrong. The best
thing that can happen is, you
might be right. I would not be
where I am today if I did not
follow my heart!"

—Shelley Zalis, founder and CEO of the Female Quotient

On *The Bold Lounge* Podcast

CHAPTER 13

DESIGN YOUR LIFE PATH

"The blueprint of a fulfilling life is drawn with actions that align with your values."

The previous chapters discussed how the first three foundational steps in The BOLD Framework—*believe, own,* and *learn*—shape your success. You are now set to move on to the fourth and final foundational step: *design*. Here you will draw on your beliefs, ownership, and learning to design your best life through a process of intentional living and personal development.

In this context, *design* refers to the deliberate and thoughtful creation of a life plan that aligns with your deepest beliefs, values, and goals. A life plan is a road map that outlines your vision for a bold future and the steps you need to take to get there. Creating a life plan involves setting priorities, breaking down your goals into manageable tasks, and establishing timelines. It is about actively shaping your life, rather than letting it be shaped by external circumstances or by default.

RECAP OF THE BOLD FRAMEWORK

Here is a quick recap about how the first three foundational steps contribute to the design process:

BELIEVE

Your beliefs are the foundational truths you hold about yourself, others, and the world. These can include your perspectives on life's possibilities, self-identity, and your place in the world. When designing your life, your beliefs, along with your values, act as guiding principles. Positive and empowering beliefs can open up possibilities, while belief conflict can constrain your potential. Recognizing and aligning your beliefs with your aspirations is crucial in designing a life that is fulfilling and authentic.

OWN

Ownership means taking full responsibility for your life and choices. It involves acknowledging and accepting that you have control over your actions and decisions, not blaming external circumstances or other people for your life situation. You have the power to recognize your mistakes, learn from them, and make proactive choices to shape a better future.

LEARN

Continuous learning is essential for personal growth and for designing your best life. It involves constantly seeking new knowledge, skills, and experiences that align with your goals and aspirations. Learning also means being open to new ideas and perspectives and using challenges as opportunities for growth. Through learning, you can more easily adapt to change, overcome obstacles, and move closer to your envisioned life.

THE DESIGN PROCESS

Using your beliefs, ownership, and learning to design your life enables you to create a personalized blueprint for a fulfilling and authentic existence. The big-picture process for designing your life plan includes the following steps.

1. **Set clear goals.** Identify what you truly want in different areas of your life, such as career, relationships, health, personal growth, and interests.

2. **Do strategic planning.** Develop a plan of actionable steps to achieve your goals, which includes setting milestones, identifying necessary resources, and creating timelines.

3. **Align actions with beliefs and values.** Ensure that your daily actions and decisions are in harmony with your core beliefs and personal values.

4. **Reflect.** Continuously assess on your progress and learn from experiences.

5. **Adapt as necessary.** Be open to modifying your goals and plans as you grow and circumstances change.

Designing your life plan a dynamic process that requires introspection, action, and a commitment to personal development. For example, Stacy, the entrepreneur from chapter 9, followed The BOLD Framework to determine and document her life path. "I used belief to propel me to design my life path, to uncover my why and the dream inside of me," she says. "I owned staying committed to keep moving forward on my journey. I owned speaking up and asking for help from others, letting go of what was no longer serving me, and learning from others, including new skills and ways of thinking and acting. The impact of ownership is transformational. I am living a life aligned with my why and my values."

With all the tools from the previous chapters, you now have a full toolbox to create the plan for your aligned and purpose-filled life. You have the power to pursue your purpose and shape your destiny. Let's explore the importance of actively participating in your journey, making your own choices, and aligning your life with your purpose and passions. It is your life, and you design it.

SHAPE YOUR FUTURE

Designing your life plan is fundamentally about making conscious choices that reflect your true self. It is a thoughtful but action-oriented construction of your future. You have already laid the groundwork by identifying your core beliefs and values. Now, you'll use this knowledge to align your daily decisions and long-term goals with what matters most to you. This isn't about grand gestures or major life overhauls. Instead, it is about making consistent, small adjustments that steer your life in the direction you want it to go. "Once I learned what I needed to change, I owned consistently committing to the small daily actions and mindset," says Stacy of her bold journey.

Designing your life is an ongoing process. Your understanding of yourself and your goals will likely evolve, and that's perfectly normal. Be ready to adapt and fine-tune your plans as you grow and circumstances change. The key is to stay connected with your core beliefs and values and let them guide your decisions. This means taking active steps to ensure that your life trajectory mirrors the things you value most.

So, as you design your life plan, approach the process with clarity and a sense of purpose. Use what you have learned about yourself as a guide to make informed decisions. By doing so, you will shape a future that is not just successful by external standards but also fulfilling and meaningful to you on a personal level.

ACTIVITY
CREATE SMART GOALS FOR PERSONAL GROWTH

In this activity, you will set specific, measurable, achievable, relevant, and time-bound (SMART) goals to design your best life based on your beliefs, ownership, and learning. These goals will guide you in making meaningful changes in specific areas of your life. The action steps and review process will help ensure that you continue to actively work toward achieving these goals.

To create your SMART goals, follow these steps.

1. REFLECT ON YOUR BELIEFS AND VALUES
Consider what is most important to you in life. Write down three to five beliefs or values that you want to focus on.

2. IDENTIFY AREAS FOR PERSONAL GROWTH

Based on the beliefs or values that you selected in the previous step, identify areas in your life where you want to grow or make changes and write them down. For example, you may want to focus on your career, education, health, relationships, or personal interests.

3. SET SMART GOALS

For each area of desired change listed in the previous step, create and write down a SMART goal. Ensure that each goal is specific, measurable, achievable, relevant, and time-bound. For example, if health is your focus, a SMART goal could be: *To improve my physical health, I will jog for 30 minutes, three times a week, for the next two months.*

4. PLAN ACTION STEPS

Break down each SMART goal into small, actionable steps. List the actions you need to take to achieve each goal. For the jogging goal, this might include scheduling time for jogging, purchasing running shoes, and plotting a suitable jogging route.

5. ADDRESS OWNERSHIP AND ACCOUNTABILITY

Plan how you will take ownership of these goals and hold yourself accountable. Decide how you will track your progress. You could use a journal, a digital app, or regular self-reflection sessions.

6. REVIEW AND ADJUST YOUR PLAN

Mark a date in your calendar (for example, in two months) to review your progress. Be prepared to adjust your goals and action steps, if necessary.

7. COLLABORATE WITH OTHERS

Consider seeking guidance from individuals who have walked a similar journey or possess valuable insights.

"Set goals that scare and excite you in equal measure, for these are the ones that ignite true change."

DESIGN PRINCIPLES IN CREATING A LIFE PLAN

The process of designing your life plan is an intentional and thoughtful approach in much the same way that architects design buildings or artists create their pieces. Let's look at some design principles that will support you in this process.

- **Vision as a blueprint:** Just as architects start with a blueprint, your life plan begins with a clear vision of your desired future. This vision is based on factors such as your deep understanding of your beliefs, values, and what you own (responsibilities, strengths) and do not own (limitations, areas for growth).

- **Iterative process:** Design is rarely a linear process. It almost always involves iterations. Similarly, make changes and refinements to your life plan as you gain insights and experience.

- **User-centric approach:** In user-centric design, the needs and preferences of the user are paramount. In the context of your life plan, you are the user. Your plan should be tailored to your aspirations, circumstances, and experiences.

- **Balancing aesthetics and functionality:** In design, you balance aesthetics (how things look) and functionality (how things work). In life planning, this translates to balancing dreams, goals, and aspirations (aesthetics) with practical steps and realistic goals (functionality).

- **Creative problem-solving:** Design often requires creative solutions. Your life plan should include strategies for overcoming obstacles and using failures and successes as learning opportunities to inform your next steps.

- **Holistic perspective:** Design considers the whole picture. Similarly, a life plan should be holistic, encompassing various aspects of your life, such as career, personal growth, relationships, health, and interests.

BRING IT ALL TOGETHER AND DESIGN YOUR LIFE PLAN

This activity will help you clarify what's most important to you, align your goals with your beliefs and values, and break down your aspirations into achievable steps. It combines reflection, strategic planning, and creativity to help you to transform your vision into a tangible, actionable life plan.

To create your SMART goals, follow these steps.

1. CREATE YOUR VISION
Start with a broad vision for your life. What are the most important things to you based on your beliefs and values? What does your ideal future look like?

2. IDENTIFY KEY LIFE AREAS
For each area, such as career or family, identify what your definition of success looks like, based on your beliefs and values.

3. DEFINE SPECIFIC, ACHIEVABLE GOALS FOR EACH AREA
Break these goals down into small, actionable steps.

4. INCORPORATE LEARNING
Reflect on how past successes and failures offer lessons that can inform your plan. Think about areas where you'd like to expand your learning.

5. OWN YOUR SUCCESS AND FAILURES
Reflect on what you have owned that has gone well and what has not gone as you expected. How can you own your steps going forward? How can you stop owning things that are not yours to own?

6. TAKE INTO ACCOUNT YOUR STRENGTHS, POTENTIAL, LIMITATIONS, AND RESOURCES

Develop achievable strategies that reflect real life.

7. REGULARLY REVIEW AND REVISE YOUR LIFE PLAN

Be prepared to make adjustments in response to new information or changing circumstances.

8. CONSIDER CREATING A VISUAL REPRESENTATION OF YOUR LIFE PLAN

This could be a physical (see chapter 12) or digital vision board, for example.

YOUR BOLD JOURNEY CONTINUES

You are the architect of your destiny. The life plan you have crafted is not just a road map. It's a reflection of your unique strengths, aspirations, and potential. It's tailored to guide you toward the future you envision for yourself. You are actively constructing a life that resonates with your deepest values and dreams.

Think of yourself as a skilled navigator. You have charted your course, but you also possess the adaptability to adjust your sails when the winds change. Your journey may not always be smooth, and that's okay. The challenges you face are not setbacks. They are opportunities to grow, learn, and reaffirm your path. You are equipped with the tools of resilience, the compass of your beliefs, and the vitality of continuous learning.

You have already taken the most crucial step: Committing to this journey and taking ownership of your life's narrative. Every day, with every small action aligned with your plan, you're not just dreaming about a future—you are actively building it. Your bold journey is a testament to your determination and clarity of purpose. As you continue forward, celebrate your progress, learn from the journey, and embrace the adventure that comes with each new day. This is your story, one that you are writing with intention and courage. You are transforming your potential into reality.

KEY TAKEAWAYS

Designing your life plan refers to the conscious and deliberate creation of your life trajectory. It involves setting clear goals, developing strategic plans, aligning actions with personal beliefs and values, and maintaining the flexibility to adapt.

A life plan includes clear goals. Identify what you want in various areas of your life and then strategically plan actionable steps to achieve those goals. This process includes setting milestones, determining necessary resources, and creating timelines. A goal without a plan is just a wish.

Align your goals and action steps with your beliefs and values. It is important that your daily actions and decisions resonate with your beliefs and values. This harmony will help you lead a more fulfilling life.

Adapt as needed. Modify your goals and plans as you grow and circumstances evolve.

Learning is a key component in life design. Continuous personal growth and adaptation to new challenges are essential and not optional.

WHAT'S NEXT

As you approach the next chapter in your journey through The BOLD Framework, you are poised to complete your exploration of the multifaceted nature of success. As part of the final foundational step, *design*, you will further refine your vision and integrate all that you have learned about yourself, your goals, and your approach to life's challenges. These refinements will help you maintain momentum on your bold journey.

BOLD MEANS

"Asking what would I do, what would I think, what would I say, who would I be if I dropped the weight of other people's opinions and expectations? For me, boldness means stepping into the fullness of everything you are—and just you, without being focused on other people."

—Alexandra Carter, mediation expert, author of *Ask for More*, and clinical professor at Columbia Law School

On *The Bold Lounge* Podcast

CHAPTER 14

KEEP MOMENTUM ON YOUR
BOLD JOURNEY

"Momentum thrives on small, consistent actions, all in tune with your greater purpose."

In the previous chapter, you kicked off the final foundational step of The BOLD Framework—*design*—and created your life plan. In this chapter, you will explore the art of preserving the momentum of your life plan, ensuring that every stride you take remains in harmony with your beliefs, purpose, and aspirations. You will learn how intentionality in action, resilience, and adaptability power this momentum.

Your journey to shape your life in alignment with your dreams and aspirations is filled with exciting possibilities, but it also demands ongoing effort and commitment. You have taken those initial leaps of faith, confronted self-doubt, and pushed through moments of uncertainty. Your progress thus far is commendable, but there will be some bumps in the road ahead. This is precisely where the concept of maintaining momentum comes into play.

DECIDE TO GO BOLD, AGAIN

Being bold is a decision that you have already made. However, maintaining forward momentum on your bold journey is not just about repeating past actions. You also need to reaffirm your commitment to your vision and adapt every single day. Daily boldness is not an isolated occurrence but a way of life. Revisit your notes from the activity in chapter 12 where you defined what you needed to do to align your beliefs and values with your goals. No one else can make these decisions and take these actions for you. It is a conscious choice to keep moving forward.

Consistent boldness nurtures momentum. For example, Marguerite, a mother of two, is passionate about writing children's books. Every morning, after getting her kids off to school, she dedicates thirty minutes to writing. This daily act of persistence, along with her courage to submit her manuscripts to publishers for consideration, keeps her connected to her dream of becoming a published author.

Still, maintaining momentum requires more than continuous action. It calls for an ongoing thoughtful process that involves self-reflection, a commitment to overcome obstacles, and an unyielding focus on your goals and aspirations. It's the realization that every sunrise brings a fresh opportunity to embrace your vision, to reaffirm your commitment to your goals.

Daily boldness means regularly assessing your journey, actions, and motivations. This helps you recognize when you veer off course and make the necessary adjustments. Daily boldness also entails a resolute determination to overcome any lingering obstacles. Challenges, setbacks, and failures can cast long shadows and create doubts about your abilities. Daily boldness is the antidote to such doubts. It's the unwavering belief that you can overcome any obstacle and the conviction that your past does not define your future.

It's easy to get distracted by the noise and chaos of life, to lose sight of what truly matters to you. Daily boldness reminds you to stay grounded in your purpose and channel your energy toward your goals. It's like a laser beam that cuts through the clutter and focuses on the target; in other words, it entails intentionality.

"Harness the power of your inner drive. It is the unstoppable force that propels you toward your goals."

INTENTIONALITY IN ACTION

Maintaining momentum requires *intentionality in action*: the art of moving forward with a clear sense of purpose, ensuring that every step aligns with your overarching goals. By being deliberate in your actions, you maintain momentum toward the goals of your life plan. Whereas momentum transforms everyday actions into calculated steps forward, intentionality is the difference between passive drifting and purposefully navigating between chaos and precision.

Intentionality requires a profound connection between actions and overarching goals. It is the conscious alignment of daily tasks, decisions, and efforts with a clear sense of purpose. For instance, in a professional context, intentionality might involve proactively seeking opportunities for growth, networking strategically, and consistently delivering high-quality work.

Intentionality in action is a driving force behind remarkable achievements. Leaders who harness it exhibit a laser-focused commitment to their goals, make decisions that align with their vision, and steer their teams toward success. Intentionality is not just about achieving goals. It's about making choices that resonate with your beliefs and values, resulting in a sense of fulfillment and authenticity.

Here's an example of intentionality in action. Anika is a sales manager and mother of two. Her overarching goal is to become the director of sales within the next five years while maintaining a healthy work-life alignment. Here's how she practices intentionality in her daily actions:

- **Strategic planning:** Each Sunday evening, Anika dedicates time to plan her week. She aligns her tasks with her goal of becoming a director. This includes setting aside time for leadership training, industry research, and project planning.

- **Networking with purpose:** Anika intentionally connects with people in her industry. She attends seminars and joins online forums to meet influencers and learn from industry leaders.

- **Quality in execution:** In every project she handles, Anika strives for excellence and innovation. She understands that her work's quality is a direct step toward her professional aspirations.

- **Aligning work and family:** Intentionality for Anika also means being present for her family. She schedules her work in a way that allows her to attend her children's important events and have quality family time.

- **Reflective practice:** At the end of each day, Anika reflects on her actions and their alignment with her goals. This helps her stay focused and make necessary adjustments.

Anika's approach exemplifies how intentionality in action transforms daily activities into strategic steps toward professional and personal goals. She moves with purpose, aligning her actions with her vision.

As Anika's reflective practice shows, intentionality in action is not static. It is dynamic and evolving. It necessitates continuous self-reflection and adaptation to ensure that actions remain aligned with your overarching goals. Adaptability, which we talked about previously and will discuss in more detail below, is a hallmark of intentionality in action that ensures that actions remain effective and purpose-driven.

Intentionality in action also fosters accountability for your choices. When you approach life with purpose and intention, you take ownership of your decisions and the outcomes (see chapter 7). This accountability empowers you to make choices that align with your goals, rather than being swayed by external pressures or distractions.

BREAK FREE FROM THE PAST

Embracing bold action and liberating yourself from the constraints of past experiences, an example of intentionality in action, is a pivotal aspect of personal growth. When you reflect on the steps you have taken on your bold journey, it becomes evident that courageous moves have propelled you forward. However, it's equally important to shed the weight of setbacks and past disappointments that may still linger.

As we've discussed, setbacks are transformative opportunities, each connected to valuable lessons. Extracting and applying the knowledge and insights they contain are integral contributions to personal growth. These experiences teach you about your strengths, weaknesses, limitations, and untapped potential. When you choose to confront your past with an open heart and a growth-oriented mindset, you transform yourself into a more capable and self-aware individual.

FOSTER RESILIENCE AND ADAPTABILITY

Your journey through life is not merely a sequence of events but a dynamic interplay between your actions and your mindset. While your actions move you forward, your mindset guides your direction. Two crucial mindset qualities that emerge as pillars of strength are resilience and adaptability. These traits are indispensable allies, especially when you confront unexpected challenges.

As we've discussed, resilience, often regarded as the bedrock of mental and emotional strength, is the capacity to bounce back from adversity. It's that innate force within you that allows you to weather the storms, endure setbacks, and emerge stronger. Resilience fortifies your resolve and empowers you to keep moving forward, even when the road ahead seems treacherous. When you possess resilience, you are not daunted by life's hurdles. Instead, you approach them with a sense of curiosity and a deep-seated belief that each obstacle is, in fact, an opportunity for growth.

Adaptability is your ability to change and flourish in shifting circumstances without compromising your beliefs and goals. This flexibility is like the agility of a skilled acrobat who effortlessly adjusts their balance while traversing a tightrope. In a world characterized by constant flux and unpredictability, adaptability ensures that you remain not just a survivor but a thriving force. It means being open to new approaches, welcoming diverse perspectives, and recalibrating your strategies as needed. You stay true to your ultimate destination while making changes as needed along the way.

THE SYNERGY OF RESILIENCE AND ADAPTABILITY

Together, resilience and adaptability form a dynamic duo that can significantly impact your bold journey and its outcome. Resilience helps you take the first step after a setback, and adaptability keeps you moving forward. Here are ways resilience and adaptability work together as you design your bold path.

- **Resilience paves the way for adaptability.** When you possess the mental and emotional strength to rebound from setbacks, you develop the confidence to explore new horizons. The knowledge that you can endure and thrive despite challenges gives you the courage to venture into unfamiliar, uncomfortable, and even scary territories.

- **Adaptability bolsters resilience.** When you are open to change and willing to adjust your approach, you become less rigid in your expectations. This flexibility reduces the impact of setbacks. You learn to see them not as insurmountable obstacles but as detours that can lead to unexpected discoveries.

Imagine encountering a sudden and unexpected problem in your career path, like a layoff. Resilience empowers you to recover from the shock and find the inner strength to act. Once you are on your feet again, adaptability comes into play. You accept the need for change, consider new possibilities, and explore different options. It's adaptability that enables you to pivot, acquire new skills, and perhaps discover a more fulfilling and rewarding career path than you initially envisioned.

ACTIVITY
REFLECT ON YOUR RESILIENCE AND ADAPTABILITY

This simple yet impactful activity will help you understand and apply resilience and adaptability. You will revisit your past experiences, analyze current situations, and prepare for future scenarios. This reflective process will deepen your appreciation of your innate resilience and adaptability and equip you with practical strategies to handle life's unexpected turns. These insights will bolster your confidence and flexibility, keeping you steady and moving forward on your journey.

1. REFLECT ON PAST EXPERIENCES

▶ Think about a past situation where you had to adapt to an unexpected change.

▶ Write down what the situation was and list the strategies and strengths you used to successfully adapt.

2. IDENTIFY A CURRENT SITUATION

▶ Choose a current situation in your life, either personal or professional, that might change unexpectedly.

▶ Write a brief description of this situation.

3. CREATE WHAT-IF SCENARIOS

▶ Imagine three different what-if scenarios that could arise from this current situation.

▶ Write these scenarios down.

4. BRAINSTORM SOLUTIONS

▶ For each what-if scenario, think of ways you could adapt, using both strategies you've used in the past and new ideas.

▶ Write down your potential solutions.

5. REFLECT ON RESILIENCE

▶ Consider the role resilience plays in adapting to these scenarios.

▶ Write down how being resilient helps you handle change and what it feels like to overcome these challenges.

6. CONSIDER KEEPING A DAILY JOURNAL

▶ To keep track of your adaptability and resilience, consider starting a daily journal or making notes in your calendar.

▶ Each day, note down small instances where you adapted well or showed resilience, including how you felt and what you learned. (If you're already keeping a journal to record your bold journey, you can add your notes there.)

NURTURE RESILIENCE AND CULTIVATE ADAPTABILITY

To nurture resilience, consider these strategies:

- **Build a support network.** Surround yourself with people who uplift and encourage you during tough times. A strong support system can bolster your resilience and provide valuable, diverse perspectives.

- **Practice self-care.** Take care of your physical and emotional well-being. Healthy lifestyle factors, such as exercise, mindfulness, and sleep, can fortify the strength needed to face adversity.

- **Set realistic goals.** While it's important to dream big, ensure that your goals are achievable. Unrealistic expectations can lead to unnecessary setbacks.

- **Learn from adversity.** Reflect on past challenges and setbacks. What did you learn from them? How did they shape you? Use these insights to develop your resilience further.

- **Use a personal affirmation.** Revisit the affirmations you wrote in chapter 9. Choose or create an affirmation that focuses on resilience, such as "I am capable of overcoming challenges" or "I grow stronger with every difficulty I face." Repeat this affirmation daily.

To cultivate adaptability, consider these strategies:

- **Remain open to change.** Be receptive to new ideas and different perspectives. Avoid becoming entrenched in fixed beliefs or rigid plans.
- **Foster a learning mindset.** Treat every experience, whether positive or negative, as an opportunity to learn. Continuously seek out new knowledge and skills.
- **Practice flexibility.** Be willing to adjust your strategies and plans as circumstances evolve.
- **Embrace uncertainty.** Life is inherently uncertain. Instead of fearing change, learn to adapt and thrive in uncertainty.
- **Seek feedback.** Regularly solicit feedback from trusted sources. Constructive criticism can provide valuable insights.

RESILIENCE AND ADAPTABILITY IN KEY LIFE AREAS

Let's take a look at how resilience and adaptability support you in three key life areas: your career, relationships, and personal growth.

Career

Resilience can be your armor against career setbacks. Job loss, project failures, or workplace conflicts are common experiences. With resilience, you can rebound, maintain your confidence, and continue pursuing your professional goals with renewed determination.

Adaptability is essential in an ever-evolving job market. Many careers today won't exist in the same form tomorrow. Factors such as technological advancements, market trends, and economic shifts constantly reshape industries. Adaptability equips you with the ability to acquire new skills, pivot into emerging fields, and remain relevant throughout your career.

Relationships

Resilience fosters emotional maturity. It enables you to navigate conflicts, handle disappointments, and recover from the inevitable ups and downs of human interactions. In personal and professional relationships, resilience helps you maintain bonds and persevere when you encounter challenges.

Adaptability in relationships includes accepting change within yourself and others with a positive perspective. People evolve over time, and so do their needs, values, and views. The ability to adapt to these changes and support others' growth is crucial for sustaining healthy and meaningful relationships.

Personal Growth

Resilience empowers you to confront your fears, step out of your comfort zone, and face life's uncertainties. It encourages you to take calculated risks, learn from your experiences, and continue evolving as an individual.

Adaptability involves being open to new ideas and experiences. It allows you to shed limiting beliefs, change your actions, and continually refine your sense of purpose. By adapting as your aspirations and values evolve, you ensure that your personal growth remains a lifelong endeavor.

"Let every action be a brick in the foundation of your future."

KEY TAKEAWAYS

To maintain momentum on your bold journey, continuously reaffirm your commitment to your vision and goals. It is a daily decision to act boldly and stay aligned with your purpose.

Embrace daily boldness as a lifestyle. Every new day is an opportunity to progress toward your goals. This daily commitment to your goals keeps you connected to your aspirations.

Regular self-reflection helps you stay aligned with your vision. Assessing your actions and motivations is vital for ensuring that you are continuing on the right path and adapting as needed.

Overcome past obstacles. Transform setbacks into learning opportunities and use them as stepping-stones toward your goals.

Maintaining momentum requires intentional actions. Purposefully align every step with your goals by making deliberate choices that resonate with your beliefs and values.

Resilience and adaptability are key to maintaining consistent progress. Resilience allows you to recover from setbacks more easily. Adaptability enables you to thrive amidst change.

WHAT'S NEXT

This next and final chapter will deepen your understanding of what it means to embody a bold mindset, an approach to life that influences how you face challenges, make choices, and engage with the world. A bold mindset infuses every decision, interaction, and challenge with courage, authenticity, and a clear sense of purpose. As you have progressed through the four foundational steps of The BOLD Framework—*believe, own, learn,* and *design*—you have been building toward this comprehensive way of thinking and being. Now, it's time to see how these elements converge to form a bold mindset. Think of this as the capstone of your exploration. It is an invitation to embark on a new chapter in your life, armed with a mindset that empowers you to live your bold life.

"Being courageous enough to push myself out of my comfort zone and into the uncomfortable."

—Amani Duncan, CEO and founder

On *The Bold Lounge* Podcast

CHAPTER 15

THE BOLD MINDSET AND YOU

"A bold mindset doesn't whisper.
It echoes through actions."

Using The BOLD Framework, you have now clarified your beliefs, decided what to own and not own in your life, embraced continuous learning, and designed your path forward. You are living a bold life.

HOW THE FOUNDATIONAL STEPS CREATE THE BOLD MINDSET

The foundational steps of The BOLD Framework—*believe, own, learn, and design*—fuse to form the BOLD mindset. This is the quintessential example of the whole being more than the sum of its parts. The BOLD mindset is a holistic approach that frees your inner boldness and unlocks your personal and professional potential. Let's look at how the foundational steps work to create the BOLD mindset.

STEP 1: BELIEVE

Belief is the internal compass that guides your thoughts, decisions, and actions. Beliefs can be limiting, holding you back, or empowering, propelling you forward.

Having a BOLD mindset starts with believing in yourself. It means recognizing your inherent worth and acknowledging your capabilities. It's about embracing the notion that you are worthy of success, happiness, and fulfillment. This belief in yourself becomes the springboard for your bold journey. The power of belief gives you confidence to determine a clear vision of what you want to achieve and hold on to that vision, even when faced with obstacles or doubts.

With the BOLD mindset, you continually challenge and reshape your beliefs. The art of belief reframing is a transformative tool. It's not about discarding your existing beliefs, but rather reshaping them to foster growth and better align with your aspirations. Your beliefs evolve as you grow, learn, and adapt. Nurturing a positive and expansive belief system opens the door to a world of possibilities.

"To think boldly is to light a fire that fear cannot extinguish."

STEP 2: OWN

Ownership entails taking full responsibility for your life, including your choices and actions. You own both successes and failures. You are the author of your story, and you have the power to actively shape its narrative by stepping into the role of the protagonist.

A BOLD mindset helps you recognize what you do and do not own by understanding the boundaries of your responsibilities and letting go of burdens that do not belong to you. A BOLD mindset also allows you to own and embrace your uniqueness. When you are unapologetically yourself, you embrace your quirks, strengths, and weaknesses, accepting that you are a work in progress. By owning your authenticity, you empower yourself to forge genuine connections with others and create a life that aligns with beliefs, values, and desires.

"Boldness is the quiet confidence that whispers in moments of doubt, 'Yes, you can.'"

STEP 3: LEARN

Learning emphasizes that every experience is an opportunity for growth. Learning also involves seeking out new knowledge and experiences and pushing the boundaries of your comfort zone. This thirst for and acquisition of knowledge feed your personal and professional development.

With a BOLD mindset, mistakes and failures are not viewed as setbacks, but as lessons and stepping-stones to success. Adaptability and resilience are essential traits of a BOLD mindset that equip you to turn setbacks into setups for success.

The BOLD mindset encourages self-reflection to examine your actions, decisions, and outcomes. It involves asking yourself tough questions, celebrating your achievements, and acknowledging areas where you can improve. Through self-awareness, you gain clarity about your strengths and areas for growth. A BOLD mindset keeps you open to daily opportunities to learn, stay curious, try new things, and engage with different people. The culmination of everyday learnings add up to significant strides toward success. Understanding the relationship between personal values, beliefs, and potential is crucial for aligning your actions with your convictions.

"Boldness is finding opportunity in every challenge."

STEP 4: DESIGN

Design your life plan is about intentionally crafting a future that aligns with your deepest aspirations. This process involves setting clear goals and creating a road map to achieve them.

You employ your BOLD mindset when you proactively shape your destiny, using a conscious and deliberate approach, characterized by clear goal-setting and strategic planning. Practicing intentionality in action strengthens your BOLD mindset, as you align every step purposefully with your goals by making deliberate choices that resonate with your beliefs and values. This commitment allows you to see each day as an opportunity to live boldly and progress toward your aspirations. With a BOLD mindset, your life is a canvas, and you are the artist.

"To be bold is to trust your own voice."

YOUR BOLD MINDSET REFLECTION AND ACTION PLAN

Congratulations on completing the journey through The BOLD Framework! You are now equipped with the BOLD mindset, which empowers you to navigate life's complexities confidently. This activity consolidates your learning and enables you to apply the BOLD mindset in your daily life. Write down your thoughts as you move through each step.

1. REFLECT ON YOUR JOURNEY

▶ Take a moment to reflect on your journey through The BOLD Framework and review the results of the activities you completed as you read the book.

▶ Think about the key insights and changes in your mindset.

▶ Revisit and highlight your favorite takeaways from each chapter.

▶ Make note of the most significant beliefs you have reshaped, responsibilities you have owned, learnings you have embraced, and design you have created for your life.

2. IDENTIFY AREAS FOR APPLICATION

▶ Consider specific areas in your life, such as personal, professional, or relationships, where you can apply the BOLD mindset.

▶ Identify one to three priority changes that you would like to make.

▶ For each change, make notes about how you can apply the BOLD components (*believe, own, learn,* and *design*) to move you forward.

3. CREATE YOUR BOLD ACTION PLAN

▶ Using your goals as your base, create and document an action plan for each change.

▶ Break down each larger goal into smaller, actionable steps and set a time for taking the first step.

4. DEVELOP STRATEGIES FOR CHALLENGES

) Anticipate potential obstacles you might face in applying the BOLD mindset to your goals.

) Prepare and jot down strategies to overcome these challenges.

5. COMMIT TO CONTINUOUS GROWTH

) Complement your action plan with ongoing learning activities, such as reading, attending workshops, or finding a mentor.

) Use what you learn to assess your progress and adjust your action plan as needed.

6. CELEBRATE PROGRESS

) Acknowledge even the small victories as part of your journey toward a bold and fulfilling life.

EMBRACE YOUR BOLD MINDSET

As you continue your transformative journey using The BOLD Framework, here are some practical strategies to guide you.

- **Challenge your beliefs regularly.** Beliefs evolve and sometimes need to be challenged. Periodically, examine your core beliefs to ensure they align with your aspirations and values. Replace limiting beliefs with empowering ones.

- **Claim ownership.** Hold yourself accountable for your choices, actions, and reactions. Surround yourself with people who encourage your growth and challenge you to take responsibility for your life.

- **Commit to continuous learning.** The BOLD mindset thrives on the belief that there's always room for improvement. Seek out opportunities to expand your knowledge, skills, and experiences.

- **Set bold goals.** Set clear and ambitious goals that reflect your deepest aspirations and values. Break short- and long-term goals down into smaller, actionable steps and create timelines for achieving them. Adjust your goals as circumstances change, but never lose sight of your overarching vision.

- **Cultivate resilience.** You will encounter challenges and obstacles. Resilience is the key to overcoming them. Resilience will enable you to bounce back from adversity with greater strength and determination.

- **Adapt as needed.** Be willing to adjust your plans and strategies as circumstances change. This flexibility will enable you to seize unexpected opportunities and navigate challenges with grace and confidence.

- **View failure as a stepping-stone.** When you make mistakes or encounter setbacks, don't dwell on them. Instead, learn from them. They are opportunities to grow and build resilience.

- **Seek support and connection.** Surround yourself with a supportive network of people who share your commitment to personal and professional growth. Share your experiences, learn from others, and offer your support in return.

- **Celebrate your wins.** Celebrate your achievements, no matter how small they may seem. Recognize your progress and take pride in your successes. This positive reinforcement will bolster your motivation and momentum.

By cultivating your BOLD mindset, you unlock your inner boldness and tap into your unlimited potential. You become the author of your story, the architect of your destiny, and the champion of your dreams. It's an invitation to live life on your terms, with steadfast belief in yourself, ownership of your path, a commitment to lifelong learning, and a clear design for the future you envision. Embrace it, nurture it, and watch as it propels you toward a life of greater confidence, purpose, and fulfillment.

Above all, remember that the BOLD mindset is not a passive state of being. It's a conscious choice, a deliberate and dynamic engagement with life. Every day is a new start, a fresh opportunity to create your story with purpose and passion. Visualize your goals not as distant dreams, but as destinations on the horizon of your journey. Each step, each decision, should be a reflection of your inner beliefs, a testament to your values, and a brick in the foundation of the bold life you are building. Your choices, whether they seem monumental or mundane, form the path to your future.

Embrace this BOLD mindset not just as a theory, but as a practical, everyday practice. When faced with decisions, ask yourself, *Does this move me closer to my vision?* When challenges arise, see them as opportunities to reinforce your commitment to your purpose. Celebrate your victories, no matter how small, for they are the signs of your bold life taking shape. Remember, the boldest story is the one you are about to write.

KEY TAKEAWAYS

The BOLD mindset begins with the power of belief. Cultivating positive, empowering beliefs helps push you forward. Continuously challenge and adapt your beliefs, replacing self-limiting thoughts with empowering affirmations.

The BOLD mindset requires taking ownership. Ownership, taking full responsibility for your life and choices, involves recognizing your power to shape your story.

Continuous learning enriches the BOLD mindset. Every experience— success or failure—is an opportunity for growth.

The BOLD mindset involves intentionally designing your life path. This means setting clear goals and creating a road map to achieve them that integrates your beliefs, sense of ownership, and commitment to learning.

Resilience and adaptability underpin the BOLD mindset. Resilience allows you to recover from setbacks. Adaptability enables you to thrive amidst change.

Maintaining a BOLD mindset requires daily reaffirmation. Choose to stay true to your vision by committing to your goals every day. Intentionality in action ensures that you purposefully align decisions with your overarching goals, turning daily activities into strategic steps on the journey to living your bold life.

BOLD MEANS

"Aligning my intentions, decisions, and actions with what's most important to who I am, my why, and my identity apart from what I do."

—Stacy Olinger, executive health care consultant

On *The Bold Lounge* Podcast

CONCLUSION

Now that you have all the pieces of The BOLD Framework, you are fully equipped with tools that you can use for the rest of your life. You have crafted a personalized guide that you can turn to whenever you want to make a change or face a crossroads, challenge, or new adventure.

With your BOLD mindset, you have the power to thrive and live the life you want. This mindset is not a destination but a way of life. You have the capability to achieve your boldest dreams and aspirations. Embrace your bold journey with enthusiasm, confidence, and the firm belief that you can shape your destiny.

The road to a bold life will have twists and turns, but it is a journey worth taking. Keep the lessons from this book close to your heart and let them guide you as you step boldly into the future. Your potential is boundless, and your BOLD mindset will be your guide on this remarkable adventure called life.

Be bold today—and every day.

AFTERWORD

As Leigh's daughter, I had a front row seat to the making of this book—from the initial idea back in 2020, when she first created The BOLD Framework, to all the writing and rewriting that led to the book you have in your hands. My mom is driven by her mission to help others in a way that inspires and empowers them to live the most aligned and joy-filled life possible. We founded Bold Industries Group with this goal in mind, and it has become the cornerstone of how we approach all that we do.

As the chief strategy officer, it has been an honor to see how the framework and company have grown over the years, positively impacting thousands of people. In addition to supporting our overall mission and vision, I lead our communications, digital strategy, and marketing endeavors. I also direct the editing and production of *The Bold Lounge* podcast and the coordination and management of our curated events.

As you can imagine, being bold is something we talk about daily, both professionally within the company and personally around the dinner table. Hearing hundreds of definitions of bold from clients and our guests on *The Bold Lounge* podcast has broadened my perspective on what it means to be bold and the wide variety of ways you can apply boldness to your life. To me, a bold act is one that is fully aligned with your truest self. It may be unpopular. It may go against the grain or the expectations of society or even those closest to you. But it is something that is important to you and feels right in an authentic way.

One of my boldest moves came a week after I graduated from college. I packed up my bags and moved seven hundred miles north to Boston. I had never lived on my own, I didn't know anyone there, and I had only been to the city a few times. It wasn't the easiest path forward, but I knew that it was the right one. The decision to move to a new place was aligned with my inner belief that I needed a fresh start, and it was important to reset and try something different. Ultimately, it turned out to be one of the best decisions I have made. That single bold move has led to transformative professional experiences, completing two graduate programs, meeting lifelong friends, and opening my entire world to new possibilities, including the decision to co-found Bold Industries Group.

Being able to work alongside someone as driven, caring, and kind as Leigh is rare and special on its own, let alone as her daughter. She gives everything to everyone else, never to herself. I am so proud to see her passion manifested within these pages.

Be BOLD Today is a guiding light for those who dare to dream and for those who seek to make a difference in their lives and in the lives of others. Its ultimate impact comes from applying The BOLD Framework in real life and the way in which it challenges and inspires you to question, reflect, and act intentionally.

The most powerful part of The BOLD Framework to me is its cyclical nature and extensive applicability.

- With each iteration, you inventory what you *believe* and then identify and reframe beliefs and values that might be limiting you.
- You *own* your missteps as much as your successes.
- You *learn* from your experiences, good and bad, and apply the takeaways to decisions.
- And it all culminates when you *design* your life—the life you want, the life you need, the life you deserve.

It is not a process that you complete only once and move on. Rather, it's a recurring journey that encourages you to look through the personal and professional areas of your life—be it your career, your relationships with others, or even the relationship you have with yourself.

Whether you are figuring out what you want, know where you want to go but don't know where to start, or you just want a particular area of your life to be better, *Be BOLD Today* can help you get there.

You have the power in your hands. By picking up this book, you have already started your journey toward being bold today.

ACKNOWLEDGMENTS

Writing this book has been an extraordinary journey filled with unexpected turns and invaluable lessons. I am deeply grateful to each person who played a part in bringing these pages to life. This book holds a special place in my heart, enriched by the support and love it received.

My special thanks to:

The Collective Book Studio team for embracing and believing in this book. Angela Engel and Elisabeth Saake: Your guidance and enthusiasm have been instrumental in shaping this journey, and I am profoundly thankful for your support and friendship.

Elizabeth Dougherty: Your editorial expertise transformed the manuscript, and I am deeply appreciative of your bold commitment.

Karen Levy: Your copyediting magic helped the boldness shine through on each page.

Rachel Lopez Metger and Carole Chevalier: Your design vision brought the book to life.

Fran Hauser: Your role extends beyond words, and I am so grateful. You helped me amplify the book's true bold message, and your support has been immeasurable throughout this process.

Bonnie Wan: I am deeply grateful for your support, insight, kindness, and friendship throughout my journey as an author. Thank you for being a vital part of this incredible adventure and believing in me.

The Bold Community: Your vibrant energy and unwavering support is at the very heart of this book. Every Bold Table, every Bold Retreat, and every interaction with The Bold Leaders Collective members and my coaching clients has fueled my passion and purpose. Your contributions are the foundation upon which this book stands. Your stories, insights, and enthusiasm have been the driving force behind every word written. I am endlessly thankful for your presence in this journey.

My incredible puppies, Yogi, Bear, Maple, and Alvin: Your unending joy, loyalty, and unconditional love have been a source of daily inspiration. Whether it's your silliness, barking to let me know the mail has arrived, or gentle nuzzles reminding me to take a break, you've been my faithful writing companions.

My parents, sisters, and brother: Words fall short in expressing my gratitude for your unwavering support and love. You've been my stronghold, the original bold tribe, offering encouragement and understanding during this journey. Your belief in me and my aspirations has been my greatest motivation. I am so blessed to have you in my life. My heart is full of love and appreciation for each one of you.

My husband, Jason: From the very beginning, you have been my unwavering pillar of strength and support throughout the creation of this book. Your belief—along with your homemade chocolate chip cookies and chai lattes—has fueled me. Thank you for your magical hugs, constant comfort, and unending love that have not only made this journey a possible one but a happy one, too. Thank you for being my partner, my best friend, and my biggest cheerleader.

My daughter, Mayah: Your presence in my life has been one of the greatest gifts, and I'm so blessed to have you as my daughter. Your belief in me has been an immense source of encouragement and motivation. The way you cheer for me and make me laugh has been my daily reminder of what truly matters, and I hope that one day you will see in this book not just my story, but also the reflection of the incredible young woman you are. Thank you for being the light in my life and for loving me through every chapter of this journey.

You! Thank you so much for picking up this book and reading it. It means the world to me. Know that I believe in you and your #bold journey ahead.

Photo: Mayah Burgess

Entrepreneur and visionary leader Leigh Burgess has inspired thousands of women and been a catalyst for empowering change in their lives. Leigh created The BOLD Framework—with its foundational steps of *believe, own, learn,* and *design*—as a guide to make real-life changes, large and small, personal and professional.

After over twenty years as an executive in health care and education, Leigh founded Bold Industries Group, a consulting, coaching, and curated-event company dedicated to helping individuals and organizations make transformative changes. She hosts *The Bold Lounge* podcast and contributes regularly to *Forbes, Fast Company,* and *Entrepreneur.*